Competition Carriage Driving on a Shoestring

D1407191

Competition Carriage Driving on a Shoestring

Jinny Johnson

J. A. Allen
London

British Library Cataloguing in Publication Data

Johnson, Jinny
Competition driving on a shoestring.
1. Horse-drawn carriages. Show driving
I. Title
798.6

ISBN 0-85131-512-7

Published in Great Britain in 1990 by
J. A. Allen & Company Limited,
1, Lower Grosvenor Place,
London, SW1W 0EL

Book production Bill Ireson

Typeset by Fakenham Photosetting Limited, Fakenham, Norfolk

Printed in Great Britain by
St Edmundsbury Press Ltd, Bury St Edmunds, Suffolk

To Thomas who has given me the confidence to drive in competitions, and to Martin who has worked so hard to get us started.

Contents

Foreword

After 40 years as a professional horseman I have not yet written my own book. I take my hat off to Jinny Johnson who started writing the book as a novice whip, and finished it as an open class driver. She has combined essential details with her own interesting entry into the sport of competition carriage driving for the benefit of others.

I know that this book will be of great interest to novice whips. By all means use it as a guide; read other books as well, but remember there is no substitute for 'miles on the clock'.

Peter Munt

List of Illustrations

Introduction

After much thought, I decided to write this handbook not to earn fame and fortune, but to help amateur drivers who are curious about competition carriage driving. I want to encourage those of you who have only ever been vaguely interested in the sport and think it might be fun, but feel you do not have the skill or know-how to take the plunge.

There can be no doubt that this is not the cheapest of sports; if you want to take part in the big national events it will involve a lot of time, dedication and money. You do not have to set your sights at this level though; more and more driving trials groups are being formed every year, who hold smaller events.

If you join the British Horse Society Horse Driving Trials section, at the start of each year you will be sent a list of all the up-and-coming affiliated club events as well as the national events. The staff at the BHS are very helpful and would be able to supply the address of your nearest club, to help you get started.

The whole of this book is based on my experience and my mistakes, and it explains the pitfalls that I came across personally. I do not intend to teach you horsecare or basic driving skills; I shall only provide information relating to competitive driving. I hope to cover everything a real beginner in the sport needs to know. I was once a complete novice and I wasted a lot of time and, probably more important, money trying to get things right. You will not learn how to become a champion driver overnight from this book, but I do hope that I can encourage you to take up what is a fascinating and thrilling sport and perhaps also save you heartache and some of that elusive stuff called money.

1 My Own Beginnings

One of the reasons that might have made you think about trying competitive carriage driving is that you can no longer ride, but the thought of giving up horses and leaving the horse world is something you just cannot bear. On the other hand, you might have been driving for several years and have lately decided that you would like more of a challenge.

I took up driving after 20 years' riding. From the age of five I spent all my time and all my money on horses. However, I eventually had to take the heart-rending decision to give up riding because of a severe hip and back problem. That day came when, after only half an hour on a horse, I could not stand the pain. When I dismounted I was unable to walk for another half hour or so because my hip had locked in one position. I knew then that I would have to give up riding.

When I was a child my father had always said that I should have a pony and trap, but somehow, at the age of nine, the idea of admitting defeat and taking up what in my eyes was an old lady's hobby was too hard a pill to swallow. Looking back now, which is an easy thing to do, I was a fool to myself and my family. I should have given up riding almost as soon as I had begun, but I tend to be stubborn and always felt that I had to prove I was as good as the next person.

At the time that I bought my first trap my husband and I were living in North Wales, halfway up a mountain. We had two small children, for whom I had bought a pony, and a donkey that had been a wedding present. I took great pleasure in leading them around the countryside but also had the itch to get myself a horse. Money was tight, but then my grandmother sold her house in order to move in with my parents, and gave each of her grandchildren a thousand pounds. Unable to contain myself, I started attending our local horse sale with the idea of buying a good steady horse that I could learn to drive with when, if ever, I had the money to buy a trap. As fate would have it, on my second outing to the sales I saw my trap. I knew at first sight that it was the one for me. It was a prime case of putting the cart before the horse!

The trap was big enough for the whole family to use – two children, my husband and me, plus the dogs. I had visions of bowling along the lanes, having picnics and going to call on friends in my beautiful turnout. It took four years after buying the cart to get out on that first drive.

The trap (I later discovered it was a Danish market cart) stood in a farmer's barn for the next two years. My husband and I moved house, onto the Cheshire plain, to be nearer a school for the children. As time went on and I was free to do my own thing while the children were both at play-school, I decided it really was time to get a horse or I would spend the rest of my life simply looking at my trap. I must admit that the more I looked at the trap the more nervous I felt about driving it.

I still had more than half of my grandmother's money in the bank, so I put the word out to friends that I was looking for a safe, 15 h.h. driving horse. In no time at all I was looking at Thomas. He was only two, broken to harness and to ride, but obviously very green. To this day I still do not know why I bought him but there was something about him that appealed to me. For the next 18 months I gave him time to grow and fill out, to find his feet and learn some manners in the stable. I bought my first set of harness, which was made out of rawhide, for £150 and began to train Thomas. I had one lesson in order to learn how to harness Thomas up and put him to. For a few weeks I long-reined him, then decided it was time for my first drive. The memory is vivid. I was so terrified that I went about a mile up the road and then turned for home. Although I can ride well, it gives you little idea of what it will be like to sit behind a horse who appears to be about a mile in front of you!

On the advice of my doctor, who also drove, I joined the local driving club where I learned an incredible amount from all the members, including a number of things not to do! It was one of the best things I did for my driving because it gave me confidence and made me appreciate how much work a horse in harness can do.

Soon pottering around the lanes on a Sunday afternoon, stopping at a pub for a drink, then trotting back to the rally host's house for tea no longer seemed very fulfilling or challenging. I let it be known among the members that if anything more exciting to do with ponies and traps went on in the area, I wanted to be included.

Eventually I was asked to help out at the carriage driving event held each summer at Tatton Park in Cheshire. Tatton Park is about 20 minutes' drive from my home. I arrived with clipboard in hand to help out at a hazard and to see the sport for the first time, and spent a wonderful two days hazard-judging and just soaking up the atmosphere. I was hooked from that moment on and for the next two years it was all I really thought about.

At that time I was in the middle of a divorce. Apart from the horse and the four-wheel market cart, which was built in about 1860, I had nothing. My harness was totally inappropriate and transport for Tom came in the shape of a borrowed cattle trailer when I was desperate. The divorce was finalised and I moved into my new home in the middle of a village with two children, cat, dogs, chickens and, of course, Thomas. By this time I had met Martin, my future husband, who spent several Saturdays converting the double garage into a box for Thomas. I was very unpopular with the neighbours when Tom woke punctually at about 5 a.m. every day in the summer and demanded his breakfast. I soon learned to wake at 4 a.m., give him a feed and creep back to bed. (I have now conquered – though not cured – this bad habit of Tom's – he lives in hobbles when in the box.)

Two years in the village centre flew by. Martin and I decided to get married and buy a house between us. The house we bought had 1½ hectares (4 acres) of land and a shed for Tom. I still had my burning ambition to take up competitive carriage driving, but I had to talk Martin into the same frame of mind. He had ridden before I met him, but had always kept his horse at livery. He enjoyed driving out on a Sunday with the club, but had never seen competitive carriage driving. I thought that as one weekend's helping had caught me, it might do the same for him and took him along to Tatton Park to help me judge. He was hooked!

We still had no transport big enough to carry both horse and trap, but we had bought a Rice trailer and Martin built a low load trailer

Our first ever attempt at driving trials. We did all three phases in this vehicle and broke the swingle tree in the process

for the trap so that we could get to all the club rallies. At that time we had two cars, both with tow bars.

We asked around at the local clubs and found that the nearby Cheshire Driving Club was holding a small one-day event. Along with three other members of our club, we decided to take part, both as individuals and as a team. Much to everyone's surprise, we won as a team and Martin and I came second in the horse class. It was enough to convince Martin and me that this was the sport for us. We kept the four-wheeled trap, and splashed out an enormous amount of money on a set of made-to-measure English leather harness for Tom.

Because carriage driving is so very time- and money-consuming, whether you compete or drive only for pleasure, it is well worth finding out how much the sport truly appeals to you before committing yourself to any great expenditure. I would advise spending time watching events and talking to competitors to discover the amount of dedication it takes to produce a turnout to competition standard. All the magazines that cover carriage driving have articles about different types of harness and their cost etc. Time spent on the study of these publications is money saved in the long run.

A few months after our triumph we went to another one-day event in Trefnant in North Wales. Our presentation was fair but we got nowhere on the marathon. We had known all along that our vehicles were not suitable (our second vehicle was also a market cart, but Swedish this time), but we just did not have the money for anything else, so we made do and broke the swingle tree in the process. All this did was convince us that by fair means or foul we would have to get hold of another vehicle.

At this point we made our first big mistake. It was October and we had decided to attend our first national event in the following May in Brighton. We should, instead, have settled on club events for that first season, but once we had set our sights on Brighton there was no turning back. Our biggest problem was transport. To use two cars was impractical as we would have no accommodation when we arrived at the event. Whether you decide to go to club or one- or two-day events, you will find it hard to manage if you have only one car and one trailer.

There are many ways around this problem. You can either put both pony and trap in the trailer (this is really only feasible if you have a pony and not a great big horse). Or, if you have a pick-up truck or a Land-rover without a cover on the back, you can put the trap on the pick-up and tow the trailer and horse. Yet another answer is to strap the trap onto the back of the trailer, but this can be a bit dangerous if you need to unload the horse in a hurry. Another disadvantage of this is that it will take the efforts of at least two strong adults. There is now a vehicle on the market that will unbolt and fit into a family estate car.

You only have to look around at these events to see that if there is a will there is also a way to transport your horse and trap: people's ingenuity is endless!

We decided to sell the Rice trailer and put our own box together. I was sent out to a farm auction to buy a wooden box, and I mean a box – no wheels underneath it, just a shell! We spent the whole of that winter either under the box fitting a new floor etc., or in the garage welding up a trap. I must add here that Martin is an engineer. He decided that the only way we could get a suitable trap together was to make one ourselves; it was just the kind of challenge he likes. We seemed to spend a lot of our time doing it ourselves.

A few weeks before Brighton I was, as I then thought, well on the way to having Thomas fit. The shell of the box now had living accommodation in it but no engine. The trap was about to have its coat of gloss paint. We could not find a chassis and cab for the box, the paint for the trap turned out to be very light green and I started to panic. Needless to say it did not stop us from going!

We hired a cattle truck and a stable on the site for Thomas and decided to ignore the colour of the trap. Martin and I, plus two dogs, slept on the floor of the cattle truck and prayed it would not rain as the roof was full of holes. I spent many hours cleaning my harness and Martin polished everthing in sight on the trap.

The late Stella Hancock to whom carriage drivers owe such a lot

I wore a borrowed grey suit of my mother's with a safety pin in the back (mother is bigger than me) and Martin wore a dog-tooth jacket with matching flat cap. With a blue and white cob, we thought we looked the part for the presentation. What a silly notion! The wonderful late Stella Hancock took us on one side after she had given us our mediocre presentation points and put us right. I could have cried after all the hard work we had put into getting there, only to find that although a certain amount of what we had done was correct, we were a long way adrift when it came to collecting those vital points in presentation.

Our dressage went well for only our third ever attempt at it. We were in seventh place after the first two disciplines. The marathon was a joke. Thomas was not nearly fit enough to start the season. Not only was the route up and over the South Downs, but as the ground there is chalk, the going was hard.

We withdrew after four hazards. It was a very hard decision to make, but I now know it was the right thing to have done. Thomas was not fit enough and it would have been a great mistake to push him beyond his capability at such an early point in his career. Although we were sad to discover so much to be wrong with our turnout we both remember that event more vividly than any other we have ever taken part in. The sun shone the whole time, we had taken part in our first three-day event, it was wonderful, and we were more determined than ever to follow this sport, come what may.

Martin and I came away from that event with such an overwhelming feeling of being made welcome. We had found ourselves part of things from the word go. As always, everyone in the sport willingly went out of their way to help and support newcomers.

2   More About the Sport

Once I had been to Tatton Park I realised that you could do more with a driving horse than just potter around or go to shows. You do not need a vast wealth of experience either on top of a horse or sitting behind it to start competing at club level. However, it certainly helps to have a good knowledge of basic horsecare and the ability to get your horse to a certain standard of fitness, although this is not so essential to begin with.

By reading on I hope that you will pick up the main points that a novice driver needs to know. One of the great advantages of driving a horse is that you can continue to be competitive for far longer than if you ride. You do not even have to be 100 per cent fit. Several people who compete are confined to wheelchairs or have severe walking problems. As long as your arms and voice are strong, you can take part. Age need not be a barrier either. Several of our four-in-hand drivers are well into their sixties – Peter Munt and HRH Prince Philip, to name but two. These older drivers are not only still competing but are still consistently winning and showing young drivers how the job is done. At the age of 62, my father has just started his first lessons, and he has never sat on a horse in his life. The only contact he has had with horses is to help me muck out my horses and ponies. So you see, anyone can take up driving and there is nothing to stop any of you from competing.

Another myth surrounding competitive carriage driving is that you must have a wonderful horse who knows it all and can show you the ropes. I do not agree with that. When my daughter first took up riding I could have bought her a pony that had won everything in sight, but I did not. I bought her a safe pony that would not throw her off at every opportunity, but was essentially green and inexperienced. Her riding improved much quicker than if she had let the pony do the job for her. She had to teach it to jump and perform a dressage test; she had to reassure it the first time it saw a coloured jump at a show. When she grew out of that first pony, I bought her a far more experienced, older one and she has won something every time she has competed with it. I believe the same thing goes for the driven horse.

The horse you propose to drive in competition should be safe, and have accepted normal run-of-the-mill things such as tractors, flags and white lines on the roads. If it will pass all of these, then I see no reason why it cannot be your first competition horse. It is unlikely to win you the Open Championship, but to start with, who thinks they will win anyway? If you did decide to buy an established winner, you could find that it knew more than you and it could end up by taking advantage of you. Unless you took enough lessons to bring your driving up to the horse's standards, you might well spoil a good horse.

A good novice horse would be a sensible buy if you do not already have one. However, if you do buy one that has had experience in the Novice Class, find out from an impartial person why that horse is for sale. Perhaps, for example, it will never go through water or has some long-established fault in its manners or temperament. A horse that consistently does the wrong thing will only destroy your confidence. Although no horse is perfect, some are definitely better than others.

For the time being, I shall assume you have a horse of some description. Let us now take a look at the four disciplines found in competitive carriage driving, together with a rough idea of what the judges are looking for.

Presentation

This is the part of the sport least liked by all drivers, but it is a very necessary evil in order to keep standards high. We were amazed at our first competition by the incredibly high standard expected. It would certainly surprise those of you who show.

Points out of ten are awarded for the following:

1 **Driver** Position, dress, hat, gloves, holding of the whip, groom
2 **Horse** Condition, turnout, condition of shoeing
3 **Vehicle** Condition, cleanliness, spares equipment
4 **Harness** Condition, proper fit, cleanliness
5 **General Impression**

Marks are only awarded in this fashion in the Novice Class. All other classes are judged on the move and it is therefore impossible for the judges to give such close scrutiny to a turnout – an incentive to move on into the Open Class!

Dressage

This section puts the fear of God into many people, but when approached in the right frame of mind it can become most enjoyable. It is true to say that the better you and your horse become at dressage, the more proficient you will become at the marathon and cone sections. For the novice driver, the relatively short test, including only a couple of circles and a few changes of gait, should present no undue worries.

Marathon

If anyone you speak to is honest, they will tell you that this is the part we all drive for. It is a real test of your driving ability, the fitness and obedience of your horse and your own mental stamina. The marathon is a cross-country drive against the clock. It includes up to eight hazards, which are also individually timed.

Cone driving

This is a test carried out after the marathon to ascertain the fitness and suppleness of your horse. It tests your ability to drive with precision at speed. In some ways this presents a challenge of the same type as the dressage test. If you learn to look at it in the right frame of mind it is good fun. You have to drive your horse through a number of special cones with balls balanced on top, set out in a twisting course. You collect penalty points every time you hit a cone and a ball falls down, and also if you take more than the permitted time.

As I have already said, the sport is run on several different levels, and I will now briefly describe the differences between the one-, two- and three-day events. In the following chapters I will describe how to work towards three-day events, as I hope you will progress to these in the future. The same skills are required at the smaller one- and two-day events as at the national three-day events. The standard of presentation etc., may not be as high at the smaller events, but if you want to do well it pays to learn the correct way of putting things together from the outset.

The bottom rung: the club-run one-day event

Some clubs omit presentation, but occasionally it is included. However, there will probably be a safety check, including a look at your spares.

You must arrive early enough at a one-day event to look at the hazards before you do anything else. At these events you are unlikely to be given a map, either of the hazards or of the marathon route, so be sure you have your own paper and pens to draw your own diagrams. As soon as you have looked at the hazards it will be time for the dressage. This will be followed immediately by the cone driving. You should then have enough time for a second or third look at the hazards.

The marathon will only be a short one of between 6 and 12 km (3½–7 miles), and do not be surprised if a considerable part of this is on the roads. If you are lucky and the club has access to open countryside belonging to some kind landowner, then some of the course will be across country.

These small one-day events are an ideal way for you and your horse to accustom yourselves to competitive work. You will find it an easy introduction to the sport, without the upsetting tension of a lot of spectators or experienced drivers watching you. It also means that you have no worries about overnight accommodation.

The next rung: the club two-day event

Two-day events are run on a much bigger scale than one-day events. They have more competitors and more helpers. The longer period of time and the larger team of organisers mean that these competitions will follow the BHS rule book more closely. In fact, this is really a mini-three-day event.

One thing that sets the two-day event apart from a one-day event is that it may include a Famous Grouse Novice Qualifying Class. What, you ask, is a Famous Grouse Class and what do you qualify for? Let me explain. Throughout the season Famous Grouse Scotch Whisky sponsors special classes, providing rosettes and helping with the running of an event by sponsoring a hazard. From every event that has Famous Grouse Sponsorship the winner of each class is entitled to take part at the National Championships, held at the end of the season. At present, these are held at Windsor Park in September. Everyone, no matter how good or well known a driver, wishes to take part in the championships. It is the biggest aim of any novice driver who has moved up from one-day events. Because of the growing popularity of two-day events, Famous Grouse has now moved some of its sponsorship of novice classes away from the larger three-day events and is helping some of the two-day events to grow in standing through its sponsorship of the Novice Horse and Pony Class.

Anyone can take part in a Novice Grouse Class at a two-day club-run event without having to be a member of the British Horse Society. However, as soon as you win your class and wish to take part in the championships, or if you wish to take part in a three-day event, then you must become a member of the British Horse Society Horse Driving Trials Group. This requires that your horse is vaccinated against equine 'flu and tetanus (a sensible precaution anyway). To find out more about this, and about your nearest events etc., contact the British Horse Society at Stoneleigh.

The disciplines at a two-day event are as follows:

24

Presentation

The judges for this section will more than likely be the same people as at a three-day event, so you will soon learn if what you are doing is correct.

Dressage

There are only three novice tests but care must be taken to learn the correct one.

Cone driving

This normally follows immediately after the dressage, but you will be given plenty of time to walk the course before you go into the ring.

These first three disciplines will all take place on the Saturday.

Marathon

This will be on the Sunday, so you have all of Saturday afternoon to look at the hazards. The marathon might well be longer than at the one-day event and it will probably include a walk section.

When you begin competing at two-day events, you have to start considering the overnight stop. When you go to spectate at any of these two- or three-day events, you will be amazed at the ingenuity people display in solving this problem. You will see temporary stables made out of just about anything that has come to hand. Often families sleep in cars and tiny tents, while the horse is given the trailer for the night.

Some people use an electrified fence to make a small paddock for the horse, and the family then move into the relative comfort of the trailer. Horses who are used to it are often tethered out for the night.

The three-day event

The following gives the running order of most three-day events, although you might find some variation on the day.

Normally this is held on a Friday, Saturday and Sunday. You and your horse must be registered with the British Horse Society Horse Driving Trials Group to take part at any national event. It is best to

25

arrive at these three-day events around Thursday lunch-time, thus giving yourself plenty of time to settle in as the *novice presentation* usually starts by 9 a.m. on the Friday. This is immediately followed by the *dressage test.*

The same three tests are used at the one- and two-day events as at the nationals. When you have finished the dressage you have the rest of the day free to look at the hazards.

The novice class is invariably the first out on the *marathon* course on the Saturday morning. At one or two of the national events *cone driving* for the novice will take place on the Saturday afternoon, but more often than not this takes place for all classes on the Sunday.

You now have an idea of the four disciplines involved and how they are organised at events. At this point I would suggest that you go along to an event and just walk around to see what people are doing. If you talk to anybody you will soon learn that everyone in this sport is friendly. No matter if they drive a team or a shaggy pony, travel Europe competing, or do one-day events near to home, everyone will help you if you have a problem and will more than willingly show you what they do and how they do it. They will let you have a look at their horse, their wagons and their stabling method.

At the three-day events the question of your overnight accommodation becomes more important. There are no rules and regulations governing how you overcome the problem of what to do with your horse while away for a couple of nights but if you do decide to progress beyond one-day events, this does become a major factor in your plans. At the three-day national events there are usually portable stables for hire but these are very expensive and if you keep the sport up, in the long run you would be well advised to make some sort of portable stabling to fix onto your trailer or lorry. By building an indoor shelter for your horse you do give yourself somewhere dry to get him ready for the presentation if it is pouring with rain.

One other, but not very advisable, way to overcome this problem is to buy yourself a lorry, make the back of the lorry into a stable for the horse and use the front as accommodation for yourselves. This might save you some time and money and avoid having to build a portable stable to fix on the side of the lorry. However, I can assure you that you will get very little sleep with a horse tramping around in the back of the wagon. Martin and I did this for the first season and a half at the national events. We appeared every morning with dark rings under our eyes and soon decided it was not for us. At the first opportunity Martin built me a lovely portable stable to go on the side of the lorry. The only disadvantage of this stable was that it took us over half an hour to erect it at every event. Martin has now perfected a portable stable that will fit onto the side of the lorry and takes five minutes to put up, thank goodness!

Is my trap/carriage suitable?

To compete under FEI rules (Federation Equestre Internationale), as in all the nationals and some of the two-day events, your trap must adhere to some very strict rules regarding weight and width. As these rules are quite complicated, and are different for horses and ponies, it is best either to buy or borrow a current copy of the British Horse Society Horse Driving Trials Rules.

For the marathon section the appearance of the vehicle does not matter one jot. As long as it is within the rules and you are happy that it is safe and will not fall apart at the first jolt, then you may use it.

You might well find that the exercise vehicle you already drive out in every day, will, with some minor alterations meet the specifications required for this. However, an exercise vehicle, no matter how much you have cleaned and polished it, would not gain you very good presentation marks, so here you face a problem. (Pneumatic-tyred vehicles are only permitted at club events.) Should you go out and buy a new, smart and perhaps antique vehicle for your presentation, and use your exercise vehicle just for the marathon? On the other hand, should you spend a lot of money on one all-purpose vehicle? A number of manufacturers provide all-purpose vehicles. One firm that has been around from the early days of the sport is Artistic Iron Products Ltd. The Bennington vehicles produced by Michael Mart and his team in Britain are constantly undergoing updating and development work. One of these is the popular back-step buggy.

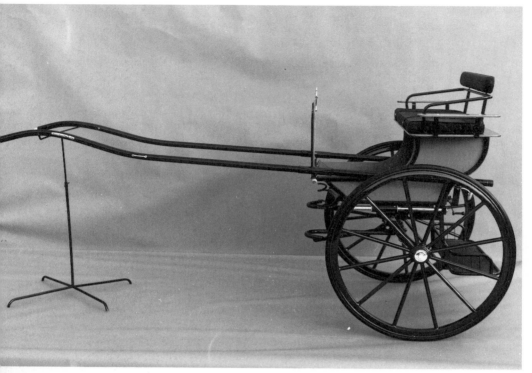

The Bennington back-step: a very popular choice of vehicle that is suitable for all three phases of competition. It is rather expensive, but the finish on these vehicles is of a very high standard

Opposite page
The Bellcrown Combi-Compact – from above to below in 15 minutes. This new design of vehicle is growing in popularity. It enables the competitor without a horse box to travel to events; half a trailer or the back of an estate car is all the room this vehicle needs when dismantled

As I have already said, one of the main problems facing the new driver is transport. One vehicle now available is the Bellcrown Combi-Compact. This has been designed for all three phases of the competition and has a great advantage in that it dismantles easily and will fit into the back of an estate car or trailer, thus helping to solve the problem of space.

Four-wheel vehicles have recently become popular for single horse and pony. Many are made with disc brakes for the rear wheels. Although the weight of a four-wheeler is similar to that of a two-wheel vehicle, the additional drag of two extra wheels gives the horse more work to do and this may not necessarily be fully compensated for by having brakes to ease the load on the horse on downhill sections. In my own view, therefore, the value of the four-wheeler for a single horse has yet to be proved, despite this vehicle's potential to make sharper turns.

If you do decide to buy a special all-purpose vehicle, then I suggest you spend some time in looking at the various makes on the market. One type will suit your requirements better than another. If the space for transporting your vehicle is limited, then you might need to remove the shafts in transit. This and many other factors must be considered before purchase.

You should bear in mind that although vehicles for the sport have been based upon traditional lines, but built with steel or alloy frames and wheels, recent developments have given further advantages. I refer to vehicles with a low centre of gravity and lower seating for the driver, plus the option of a back step. Such vehicles give a competitor the ability to go faster safely in hazards. Four-wheel vehicles will, of course, have higher seating, to allow the front wheels to pass under the body when turning, and a higher centre of gravity.

Do I have to change my harness?

The rules do state that any harness that is clean and well fitting will do for every part of the competition. You would be well advised, however, to think about getting two sets of harness, one for the presentation, dressage and cone driving, the other for the marathon. The type of harness you buy is, of course, entirely your own preference; there are now so many different varieties on the market that it can be quite a bewildering job to make a choice. I can only make a few suggestions that might be of some help.

For the presentation, dressage and cones, I would recommend that you consider buying a leather set. This can be either ordinary leather or patent leather. You can buy ordinary leather in black or brown, with brass or chrome fittings. If you have a lovely liver chestnut horse, it might look better in a brown set; there again, if you have a snow-white horse it could look better in a black set.

Very smart, strong, easy-to-clean webbing sets are now also widely used, but be sure to buy a reputable make.

Bridle, breast collar and saddle pad of handmade English leather

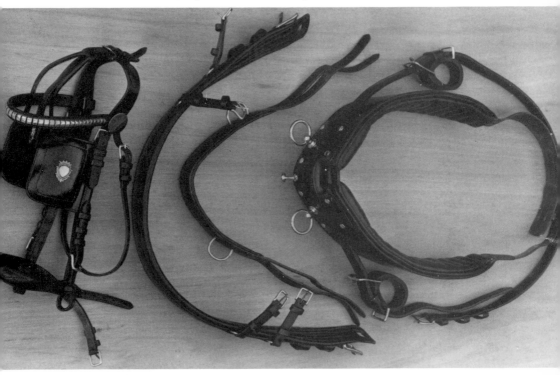

The Dura-web as supplied by Tedman Harness. This is rubber-coated webbing harness and comes with brass or black buckles. It is very strong, and suitable for the presentation/dressage and the marathon

The question of what to buy for the marathon is even more bewildering. With so many different makes of webbing harness and leather sets on the market, it can be very difficult to know what to start looking at. I would suggest that you examine harness that your friends might have bought. Some of the webbing harness is now so well reinforced, and may also have leather in certain parts, that it will last almost as long as a traditional leather set. My own personal preference is for chrome leather as supplied by Don Carney of Macclesfield. This is as easy to care for as the webbing set as it only requires washing off after use. An occasional saddle-soaping is all that is needed, and for somebody as lazy as I am, this is a boon.

Even if you already have the correct harness and vehicle, getting the whole thing ready for competition is a totally different matter. No amount of money or time spent in watching experts executing a marvellous dressage test can prepare you for your first event. At every stage you will have a multitude of questions to ask. The reply most readily given in a rush is to look in the rule book. If you have already joined the British Horse Society Horse Driving Trials Group and have read the rule book, you will know that finding the relevant answer can be like looking for a needle in the proverbial haystack. Have you tried to read it to find out what a good presentation is? Or how to produce a good collected trot, for that matter? Unless you have ridden you probably do not know the difference between working and collected trot anyway.

When trying to work out your first set of hazards, you will end up with a diagram looking as though you have just had an attack of the shakes, and just when you think you have everything under control some bright spark will remind you that you do your cone driving at some unearthly hour the next morning and you really should go and walk the course for the first time now – in the dark!

The only answer to all these problems is, of course, experience. By all means take all the advice you can get, but an ounce of knowledge acquired by doing it yourself is worth a ton of help.

I do not profess to know everything there is to know about competitive carriage driving, or to have won hundreds of events, but Martin and I have spent the last three years learning by our mistakes and have had the pleasure of being placed in almost every novice event and open class we have taken part in.

If you have only ever watched a couple of events, some of this will still be double Dutch. Perhaps my suggestions will help to shorten your time of trial and error; perhaps those of you who have been thinking you might give this sport a try will actually take the bull by the horns, or the horse by the reins, and have a go. The ultimate aim of us all might be to drive the perfect team or pair, or come out with the best dressage score ever, but I think the most important thing is to take part, enjoy yourself and have fun with your horse. To improve your scores gradually as your first season progresses is a sensible aim. Don't bank on coming out a winner to begin with.

3 Fitness

The fitness of your horse is one of the most important things to learn about. The dos and don'ts of the four disciplines are mostly a matter of reading the rules and changing old habits for new, but if your horse is not properly fit and therefore healthy, you will stand little chance of doing well in any part of competitive carriage driving. It takes a lot of hard work and self-discipline to get a horse really fit and there are no short cuts or easy ways to do it.

What is a fit horse?

A fit horse is one that can do the job you ask of it without any adverse effect on its health. It should be able to cover the distance you ask at the speed you need without becoming distressed. It should look comfortable and happy after hard work and not stand heaving and sweating.

How do you know when a horse is fit?

In 1988 the British Horse Society Horse Driving Trials Group engaged the Animal Health Trust of Newmarket to carry out research into the stress to which horses are exposed during the marathon stage of a driving trial. The findings were very interesting and it was a pleasant surprise to learn that a fit horse would suffer no undue stress or damage to bodily tissue on the marathon. You can obtain the original report from the British Horse Society Horse Driving Trials Office. However, below I shall give the bare bones of the subject, which should be enough to give you confidence during your early years.

Dr David Snow, who led the project, has given some guidelines by which to measure the fitness of a horse or pony during training. These depend on knowing the pulse rate, the breathing rate and the body temperature at various stages in a cycle of activity from resting through hard work and back to rest. For simplicity, it is possible to use the pulse rate and the breathing rate on their own. If they are showing satisfactory values, then the body temperature will usually be found to be within safe limits too. (The rectal temperature is somewhat tedious to measure in the practical world we are describing.)

The pulse rate is measured by placing your fingers underneath the jaw bone and counting the number of beats per minute in the artery that crosses the bone there.

Respiration is assessed simply by watching the movement of the horse's sides as it breathes. An in and out movement counts as one breath.

For both sets of measurements it is accurate enough to count the number observed in a quarter of a minute and multiply this by four to find the rate per minute.

Normal resting heartbeat is 30–40 beats per minute (b.p.m.). Normal resting breathing rate is 10–20 breaths per minute (b.p.m.). The maximal heart rate of horses and ponies is 230 b.p.m.

The research, which had the benefit of using a heart monitor, showed that 230 b.p.m. was reached for only one or two minutes at a time during the marathon when the horses were hill climbing or negotiating a hazard. During the trotting phases heartbeat rates in fit animals were usually 150–180 b.p.m. This returned to 40–50 b.p.m. at the halts on the marathon. At the finish of the marathon, rates of 150 b.p.m. were recorded in horses and 184 b.p.m. in ponies. These usually fell rapidly over 10–15 minutes.

The length of time it takes for your horse's pulse and breathing rates to fall from the high figures achieved when working hard to the low figures applying at rest, is the most reliable guide to its fitness.

A practical test of fitness is to measure the time taken for recovery from 150 b.p.m. heart rate down to half this rate or one and a half times the horse's resting rate, whichever appears to you to be the best indicator of when it is comfortable. The shorter this time becomes, the fitter the animal is.

Do not expect to find pulse rates in your horse of 220 – the maximum you are likely to count is 160, i.e. 40 beats in a quarter of a minute. By the time you settle into your full training regime, this should settle to 60 or below after a five-minute level walk.

Getting your horse fit

No horse can become truly fit living out at grass. Grass is the basic food of the horse, but it cannot attain more than a basic level of fitness eating grass alone. You can keep it at grass and feed it supplements, but very few horses know when to stop eating. They will browse for most of the day and night and become far too fat.

A horse that is overweight is going to struggle when pulling you, a trap and its own heavy body around. It may seem cruel to shut it up during the summer, but it is the only way to get anywhere with its training. You must be strong-minded and bring the horse in from the first day of training. It will soon get used to it and you will get used to the idea that you are helping the horse by monitoring what it eats.

Some horses can suffer from respiratory problems when they are stabled all the time. Some will also pick up bad habits. We will look at these problems before we go any further.

Respiratory problems

Respiratory problems may stem from an allergy to the bedding you use or to the small fungal micro-organisms that live in the dust in hay. If you find that your horse is coughing when he is in the box, you can try to eliminate whatever is causing the cough yourself before you call in a vet for advice.

Hay allergy
No matter how good your hay is, try soaking it for at least 12 hours before feeding. It is often recommended that you soak hay for 24 hours to prevent fungal spores becoming airborne, but you might find that 12 hours are sufficient for your horse. You will not have killed the micro-organisms etc., but you may find that if you get rid of the dust that floats around when the horse pulls at its hay net, that

is enough. If the cough persists after a 12-hour soak, progress to 24 hours and see if there is any improvement.

After trying the soaking method, you could try feeding pre-packed hay. This is sold under several brand names and comes in large plastic sacks and has been compressed so that it looks rather like silage. It is more expensive than ordinary hay but may be higher in protein so you will not need to feed so much. If you do decide to try this form of hay, ask your supplier how much to feed your horse. It can be very harmful if fed at too high a rate. This form of hay goes off quickly once the bag is opened, and care must be taken not to feed it once it has begun to ferment.

Bedding allergy
After trying to eliminate the coughing problem by looking at a possible hay allergy, the next thing to look at is your bedding. Straw will carry as many micro-organisms as hay, so try to change that first. Shavings are widely used as bedding. They might appear to be much more expensive than straw, but if you build up a reasonably deep litter they work out cheaper in the long run.

When you first put down a new bed of shavings a lot of dust will fly around. If you use a hand-held spray (or a *clean* one of the type sold for use in the garden) to give the bed a light cover of water, this will hold the dust down until the bed is a bit soiled and the dust settles itself. When you add new bedding, mix it in with the old and leave the door open for a while.

A satisfactory non-allergic type of bedding is shredded paper, but this can be hard to obtain and is a bit difficult to live with. If you still have no joy in eradicating the cough through these simple home remedies, you would be well advised to seek the help of your vet. For horses with very bad allergies there is now a Ventolin inhaler, but this is only for the most severe cases. Always remember that poor hay in the nextdoor stable, or in the loft above, can also affect a horse that is sensitive to fungal spores.

Boredom in the stable

One of the main worries of someone with only one horse that is stabled all the time is the fear of bad habits developing. Think what you would feel like shut up all day. You would probably start to chew the woodwork or kick the walls. Your horse feels just the same.

If you can manage it make sure that your horse is given as many small feeds a day as you can manage. The highlights of any horse's day are feed times; feeding little but often aids the horse's digestion and fills in the day.

Many horses will play if given a football or a couple of buckets with the handles taken off. They will kick these around or even pick them up and toss them in the air. My horses listen to the radio for several hours a day and do seem to enjoy it.

Some variation to routine

Although you wish your horse to be in the stable most of the time in order to restrict its grass intake, it will do it the world of good to spend an hour a day out in the field. It gives it a chance to roll and have a good play, especially if it has company. This should also keep the horse from becoming stale and perhaps help to prevent it from acquiring bad habits in the box.

I always give my horses a regular day off. This gives me a chance to catch up on the housework and gives them a well-earned rest. Try to make the rest day the same day every week. Horses like routine. Because they are having a day off does not mean that they should go out for the whole day – a couple of hours in the middle of the day will be plenty of time for them to relax. The night before their day off, be sure not to give the normal amount of feed; they will not be working and so do not need to eat so much. A simple bran mash with some apple or carrot would do.

To clip or not to clip

Although you will have had your horse fit enough for normal pleasure driving, it will probably never have been fit enough to undertake some of the marathons you will encounter, even at a two-day club event. You now have to look at fitness in a new light. You are training the horse to be as fit as a horse that hunts twice a week and must build up its stamina and staying power. This is impossible with a thick winter coat.

Before you can start a real programme of work with a stabled horse, you must, therefore, get rid of this coat, otherwise, after only a small amount of work, the horse will begin to sweat and become uncomfortable. The easiest solution is to clip the coat off thus achieving an immediate reduction in sweating and the consequent loss of condition you are trying to attain. If for some reason you cannot clip your horse, rugging it up in the stable will encourage the shedding of the winter coat earlier than normal; you cheat it into thinking spring has come early.

In my opinion, clipping is the best way to start working a horse in the early spring, but by using the rugging method it is possible to start training a little sooner than you may have done in the past.

Weight

As soon as the horse comes in, you are in control of what it eats. Your aim is to get its weight down (assuming that, like most horses that have just spent the winter out at grass, it is carrying around a very large tummy). This fat will come off as you start to exercise, but if you feed too much the horse will be unable to work well or to lose weight. When it reaches its peak of fitness you should be able to see (in the majority of horses) a definite line between its stomach and rib cage, it will do no harm if you can almost see its ribs. A horse that is overweight has a very hard job to do. The more weight it carries the hotter its internal organs will become. The hotter the horse gets inside, the harder it is for it to work. Its insides need to be able to cool as quickly as possible. The less fat it carries, the less insulation it has, therefore it will cool more quickly and work more efficiently.

What, and how much to feed?

When Dr David Snow carried out the tests during stress on the marathon, he also looked at feeding rates likely to help attain the correct level of fitness. His findings are given below.

A guide to the weight of food in kilograms required daily can be calculated by multiplying the horse's height in hands by 0.8. This works out at 11.2 kg for a 14 h.h. pony, 12 kg for a 15 h.h. horse and 12.8 kg for 16 h.h. The type of food will depend on the work being

39

done. The more work being done, the greater the proportion of concentrates that you will need to feed.

	Percentage of diet Hay	Percentage of diet Concentrates
Maintenance only	100	0
Light work	70	30
Hard work	50	50
Fast/endurance work	30	70

Therefore, the 15 h.h. horse will take 12 kg hay at rest, 8.4 kg hay and 3.6 kg concentrates in light work, 6 kg hay and 6 kg concentrates in hard work, and 3.6 kg hay and 8.4 kg concentrates in fast/endurance work.

On a more scientific basis the energy requirement for maintenance is calculated by adding 18 to $\frac{1}{10}$ of the horse's body weight in kilograms, i.e. for a 400-kg horse this means:

$$18 + \frac{400}{10} = 58 \text{ MJ}^*$$

The following table gives the energy and protein values of some commonly used feeds.

	Energy value MJ/KG	Protein level %
Poor hay	6–8	average, around 7% but can vary
Average hay	9	
Good hay	10–11	from 12–18
Horse and pony cubes	10	10·5
Beet pulp	11	9
Oats	11	11
Barley	13	14
Racehorse cubes	13	14
Maize	14	9
Sugar lumps	16	0
Corn oil	36	0

* The megajoule [MJ] is a unit of energy.

The amount of energy required for work is difficult to calculate, but a light endurance horse in hard work is thought to need approximately 200 MJ/day, and successful racehorses in training are routinely fed 160–210 MJ/day. It can be seen from the above that the maintenance requirement for the 400-kg horse can easily be met by 10 kg of moderate hay, i.e. two average haynets.

However, as soon as it steps out of the stable the demands go up, and to provide the 200 MJ/day required in hard training/competition, the same horse would have to eat 20 kg of top quality hay. As the maximum daily intake is 3 per cent of body weight, i.e. 12 kg, this is plainly impossible, so higher energy feeds must be used. The energy yield of grains (oats and barley) is increased by up to 3 per cent by bruising or cooking. Fat, in the form of vegetable (corn) oil, can be added to make up the energy shortfall, up to a level of 20 per cent of the daily total weight of dietary intake.

The mature competition horse requires no more than 8 per cent dietary protein. However, this protein should be of good quality and supply the amino acid protein components in sufficient variety and quantity essential in horse nutrition, e.g. lysine and methionine are two of the three essential amino acids. Feeding over the 8 per cent level is wasteful and potentially harmful. The table above shows that more than adequate levels are available in all traditional horse feeds (except very poor quality hay) and also indicates the value of feeding fats.

ADAS (the Agricultural Development and Advisory Service branch of the Ministry of Agriculture) can analyse hay and feed samples, and it is well worth checking with them to avoid overfeeding. Horses and ponies, just like humans, are all individuals and must be treated as such. Consequently, these guidelines need to be adjusted to suit the individual animal's needs.

Salt in the diet
It can be easy to overlook the amount of salt a horse will lose through sweating. Even with its coat off and a steady increase in work, the horse is bound to sweat. It will lose fluids and salt. You will probably have a salt lick in the box, but many horses will not use this.

To make sure the salt level is kept up, give the horse two level tablespoons of ordinary table salt every day it is in work. This will also encourage the horse to drink a bit more, thus keeping up fluid levels. Check, however, that this salt is not already being supplied in any mineral supplement that you are adding to the feed.

Your exercise regime

With the coat off and a new diet begun, it is time to start the exercise regime. The impression that many people have is that if we cover so many kilometres a day for so many weeks on the run then that must make a fit horse. This is not strictly true. You do need to clock up quite a lot of kilometres to get a horse fit, but by making your horse work harder when it is out you can reduce the distance you cover and cut down on time spent in the trap.

Week I

Start your training by walking the horse for no more than 3 km (2 miles) a day for at least the first four or five days. One of the reasons for doing so little to begin with is that it takes time for the muscles and tendons of the horse's legs to harden.

It would be wonderful if we all had access to cross-country tracks or all-weather surfaces but, unfortunately, most of us have to use roads. Great care must be taken at this early stage of training. If you are preparing a young horse for his first season, then even greater care must be used.

If you start trotting from the first day the horse will more than likely develop sore legs (concussion damage) and harness galls may also appear. If you know your horse is prone to soreness (especially on the point of the shoulder and under the girth), you can rub this area with ordinary toilet soap, then surgical spirit followed by a dusting of talcum powder. Make sure that this does not set up an allergy by testing it first for a couple of days on a small patch of skin that does not come into contact with the harness.

Another old-fashioned, but very effective, method of preventing galls is to dab human urine onto the areas that may become sore. This works because urea and other chemicals in the urine react with the horse's skin and cause it to harden

If you find that your horse has developed a sore, you can treat it with salt water (this also helps to harden the skin), but prevention is always better than cure.

Week 2–3 or 4

Gradually increase the distance you cover in walk. After the first week or two you can spend some time in trot – about two minutes at a time to start with. After perhaps the middle of the third week, when you are sure the horse is happy with this light work, you can begin to think in earnest about fitness training.

Week 4 onwards

If you have a date in mind for your first competition of the season, you must set aside at least ten weeks for your fitness training. If you can give your horse an extra couple of weeks then do so. The longer you can take over getting fit, the better as you will not rush your horse. The slower you take things the more completely fit your horse will be.

After the initial three to four weeks of mainly walking with short trots in between, you can make an effort to get more work out of the horse. When you are out, make it work properly all the time. Only let it walk on a long rein when it is almost home; the rest of the time make it walk in a positive manner. Take up more contact with the reins and push the horse onto the bit with your voice or a crack from the whip.

Make the horse do the same in trot. When it is only in its normal working trot it is not using itself enough. If you make the horse collect itself, it will use more muscles and energy, and will therefore work harder and need less time out on the roads.

As you slowly increase the training period, stick to the work pattern of work in trot (properly) for four minutes at a time. After each trot, walk the horse on in an active fashion until its breathing is back to normal. As time goes by, the breathing will return to normal faster and faster. When you can be out driving for, say, 45 minutes using this method and you are happy that the horse is coping well and is still a bit fresh at the end of your drive, this is the time to start to push that little bit harder. You can now trot for longer periods but continue to let the horse have a good walk in between. By always letting it walk, even though you are making it walk out well, you are slowly increasing its capacity for work and its staying power.

Increasing power from the quarters

Now you must increase the horse's power; this comes from the hindquarters. If there are any hills nearby then this is the best area in which to continue the training (and hardening off) of your horse. Start by finding a slope that is not too long or steep, and walk up it to begin with. Do not let the horse stop while going up or when it reaches the top.

Make sure that the horse is really walking well and using its hindquarters. Do not let it drop its head completely. It will need to lower it to some degree, but by making it hold it higher than it would normally do, you are ensuring that the hindquarters are working. When you are sure the horse can cope with this at walk, then start to trot up. If the horse gets tired halfway up, let it walk but do not let it stop. As you gradually find that it can manage this in trot and can then trot for another 100 metres or so, then, and only then, look for steeper slopes. Always remember to walk between trotting sessions until the horse's breathing is back to normal. Try not to spend more than an hour and a half to two hours out at a time. If the horse is working well, this is more than enough for regular training drives.

If you have no hills to work on, try to find some rough tracks or fields. The wheels of the trap will sink slightly into mud or grass (or, even better, sand) so that your horse will have to work much harder to cover the ground than when it is on the roads. As almost all of the marathon section will be on tracks and across fields, even at club level, it is well worth finding somewhere to practise this kind of driving, even if you have to box up your horse to get to it. By doing some of your driving across tracks etc., you will also be getting some practice yourself at how to steer on rough ground.

You should have taken about ten or twelve weeks to get to this point, depending on the type of horse you have and how much work it is used to. When you can happily be out for an hour and a half and your horse still seems to be reasonably fresh on the return home, then you know that you are about ready to drive at an event.

I would suggest from now on that once or twice a week you push your horse a bit harder. Make it trot for longer periods at a time, but take care if this is all on the roads or very hard ground because constant concussion can lead to problems, e.g. 'jarring up', or splints in young horses.

When you are out on your training runs, as well as trying to choose as many different routes as possible, try to spend, say, 15 minutes a week practising going through cones or hazard driving. You do not need a flat field for this or even to have a hazard set up; a few road cones set up in the shape of a hazard are all you need.

To get your eye in for cone driving, all that you will require is a set of six or eight cones. Set them out, giving yourself 30 cm (1 ft) clearance beyond the track width of your vehicle and drive in any

When a pony is long-reined it has to work very hard. A ten-minute session of long-reining is better than no exercise at all

45

order. Do not spend too much time on this or your horse will soon realise what it is supposed to do and try to dash through them.

What happens if you are unable to get out to drive?
Missing up to two days' work will not do any harm to your horse or the training routine. However, missing more than this can set you back by as much as four or five days. If you do not always have time to drive out, then try to give your horse two short sessions of long-reining or lunging. Your time is better spent giving the horse exercise than grooming it.

Simple rules for fitness
Start slowly, be patient for the first two weeks.
All walk and trot work should be active and on the bit.
Walk between every trot until breathing returns to normal.
Gradually increase work uphill and over rough ground.
Keep up salt and fluid levels.
Feed for work yet to be done, not what was done the day before.
A slimmer horse is, nine times out of ten, a fitter horse.

4 Presentation

The presentation is the first discipline and, as I have already said, it is the one least enjoyed by most competitors. It is not usually found at one-day events but is always part of a three-day event and more often than not included in a two-day event.

In the interests of maintaining a high standard of driving, the presentation is a good way to make sure that everyone who competes is able to produce a horse and turnout to a corresponding level of appearance. A horse that is fit and well will look good at its presentation and should gain you good marks to begin with. It naturally follows that if a horse is unfit and not 100 per cent in health, it is not going to give a good performance.

This is a bit like saying if you cannot pass the starting post you should think twice about going on any further.

Scoring

The scoring is written down on a sheet that is set out in columns, with one space for each part of the turnout to be marked. The highest mark awarded by each judge is 50. All the judges' marks are then added together and divided by the number of judges. (This can be two, or sometimes three.) These points will be deducted from 50. This result is then divided by five to give the penalty points. The competitor with the lowest number of penalty points will be placed highest.

The horse

Looking at the score sheet is one thing, achieving what is required is quite another matter. You must begin your preparation for the

COMPETITOR NO	TO BE JUDGED	MARKS 1 — 10	REMARKS
1. Driver, Groom and Passengers	Position, dress, hat, gloves, holding whip, handling of horses.		
2. Horses	Condition, turn out, cleanliness, matching, condition of shoeing.		
3. Harness	Condition, proper fit, cleanliness.		
4. Vehicle	Condition, cleanliness, height of pole and spare equipment.		
5. General Impression	Whole turnout.		
	TOTAL PRESENTATION		

SIGNATURE OF JUDGE ....

Judging sheet: Competition A, Section I

presentation the moment you first bring your horse in for the summer. I will assume that the horse is clipped out, but if it has a lot of feathering on its legs, you may well have left this on – it is an entirely personal decision. However, this may give you more to do at the last minute.

Some of the beauty treatment cannot be done until the week before an event, as various parts of the coat and the whiskers will grow back quite quickly. The things that you can do well in advance of a competition are as follows.

The mane

The mane must lie on the right-hand side of the neck. You are luckier than you know if your horse's mane already does this. The first step is to wash the mane and comb it out onto the right-hand side. The type of horse determines what length of mane is suitable. For a horse that has Thoroughbred or some such fine blood in it, you need to aim for a short neat mane that will plait up. Native breeds can be left with long manes but even these should hang on the right and be tidy. If your horse is just a cob type, then pull the mane to about 15 to 20 cm (6–8 in) long. To make the mane lie on the right, put it in tight plaits, taking the mane from an area along the crest of about 10 cm (4 in) into each plait.

You will have to put the plaits in every day to make sure that the horse is unable to rub its mane. After several weeks you should find that you can leave the plaits out for a day or so, but as soon as you see the mane trying to flick back over to the left, put the plaits in again.

If you find that you have a really stubborn mane, then you would be better off washing it the day before an event and putting it into bunches. These will keep the mane on the correct side but will not leave it looking as though you have just taken it out of the curlers. On the morning of the presentation, leave the bunches in until about an hour before you are due for your presentation, then give the mane a vigorous brushing. For all but the most persistently wiry manes, this should keep it in place long enough to ensure no marks are lost.

If you go to horse equipment sales, you might find a pair of mane layers (these are rather like hair grips for horses). They are made of wood and metal and fasten onto the mane, holding it on the correct

49

side by their weight. They may be old-fashioned but they do the job. If all else fails, you can hog the mane.

The tail

All horses' tails, rather like their manes, do their own thing unless trained otherwise. To make the tail smart, and to show the horse's back end to the best advantage, cut the tail about 20–30 cm (8–12 in) below the hocks. If you make the first cut about a month before your first event, and then trim it several times, it will look thicker at the end.

The top of the tail will either look like a scrubbing brush or be as smooth as silk and lie flat without you ever having to do anything to it. If it resembles a scrubbing brush and is very thick, you can either pull it, or take a razor to the edges. Unless you already know how to do either of these things, you are better off leaving this to a friend or freelance groom. It is better to pay someone a couple of pounds than end up with no tail!

The tail, like everything else, must be very clean. I do not use horse shampoo because both my horses have so much mane and tail that to buy special shampoo would cost a fortune. I buy the biggest and cheapest bottles of shampoo I can find at the supermarket and although Tom might smell a bit sweet, he certainly looks clean.

If you have a horse with a white tail, it is more than likely to soil it in the horse box on the way to an event. A bandage might stay on the top half of the tail but it is quite likely to fall off the end. To keep the tail clean in transit, I use the leg of an old pair of woollen tights. I put the tail into the leg of the tights and secure it with the tail bandage. This will not only keep the tail clean but means you do not need to plait or knot the tail to stop it getting tangled up.

The legs

If your horse, like Tom, is definitely a cob with a great deal of feather, then leave the feather on. Take a pair of scissors to the backs of the legs and tidy up around the knees to about halfway down the cannon bone. Keeping the feathers looking good is hard work as they tend to get very greasy. The only way to achieve this is a lot of hot water, shampoo and elbow grease! To keep the legs clean during transit, you can bandage them with some gamgee or foam under the bandage. You might find that your horse is prone to sweat during the journey so that its legs become sticky and need washing again. Try putting hay or straw under the bandage; it will absorb the sweat and keep the legs dryer.

If you do decide to take the clippers to your horse's feathers you are certainly giving yourself a much easier job when you come to getting ready for presentation, especially if the legs are white, as Tom's are. However, even if you do take the feather off, you must get the scissors out before every event and cut off any bits of hair that are looking long and tatty. If you do clip the feathers off, I can assure you it will be more than two years before they grow back looking silky as they did originally. So if you do decide to clip them, you will probably have to clip them every season.

Whether your horse has a lot of feather or not, the legs must be clean and all stray hairs from the back of the legs must be removed. If your horse has only a bit of fluff around the bottom of its legs, you would be well advised to clip this off. The horse will look much neater with either totally clean legs or full feather, not half and half.

The shoes

Your horse's shoes will be given close scrutiny and you will definitely lose marks for feet in poor condition. Try not to have a new set of shoes put on just before an event; shoes are very heavy and take a good week to bed into the foot. Your horse needs to be well shod but if this is done too close to an event you run the risk of:

(a) a shoe coming off because it has not had time to bed down;
(b) tiring your horse needlessly on the marathon because it has extra weight to carry around. (This is no laughing matter if it has old-fashioned shoes like Tom.)

Talking about the shoes leads on to the question of studs. As most of my work is on the roads and many of them are very steep, I have studs on both my horses. They have one small stud permanently in each shoe (protruding 2 or 3 mm, *not* the large screw-in type). Once you have put in studs you must always do so; it is unfair on the horse

51

to give it non-slip soles one day and then take this support away the next. Your farrier is the person to consult on this, as he is the expert.

The following jobs must be done on the morning of the presentation or a couple of days before an event.

The head

Your horse will have long whiskers on its chin and around its muzzle, all of which need to come off. You can use scissors, a safety razor or hand clippers for this. Tom is quite used to being shaved and will almost fall asleep while I do it. From the chin to the throat there will be many long thick hairs that hang below the jawbone. Use clippers or scissors to remove these as well.

Hair grows out of the ears in tufts. Take hold of the ear from behind and close your hand around it. You can then cut off all the hairs that stick out. Never cut the hair inside the ears as this protects the horse from flies, but the tufts that stick out are not needed.

None of these things are harmful to the horse and they will not hurt him unless you happen to take a slice out of him!

The last thing to do on the day is to wipe the eyes and nose with a damp, clean sponge. As a finishing touch put some baby oil onto your hand and rub this over the muzzle – the horse will gleam with health.

Note: When out at grass, the whiskers around the horse's mouth act as a form of sensor to protect the nose. Regrettably, most judges suggest these should be taken off for presentation purposes.

The feet

Do not pick out the horse's feet on the morning of the presentation until it is out of the box and ready to be put into the trap. If you pick out the feet in the box, they will collect shavings, straw or muck, and then you will not be able to oil them. When the feet are clean and free from mud inside and out, you can oil them both inside and outside. The judge for the presentation will pick up one of your horse's feet, so you must make sure that all the feet are clean and oiled. Some horses are not very keen on having their feet picked up when they are in harness, so this is a useful lesson to practise at home.

The mane and tail

Keep the tail bandage on for as long as possible, then give the bottom of the tail a quick brush out just before you remove the bandage. If you have had to put bunches in the mane, take these out in enough time to give the mane a good brush with a soft body brush.

Finally, the horse must be spotlessly clean, without a stable mark in sight, and its mane and tail hanging like silk.

Last-minute checks for the horse

On the morning of presentation, in plenty of time, check that:

All whiskers on the face are shaved.
There are no stray hairs on the legs, especially on the heels.
The feet are oiled inside and out.
Stablemarks on white hocks are covered by chalk. (You can buy this at a saddlers.)

The harness

Because competitive carriage driving is judged on the overall performance of the horse and not on how much money you have spent on your harness etc., you should be able to do your presentation in any harness that fits your horse correctly and is strong enough to withstand the rigours of a marathon.

The rule book states: 'For competition A and C [presentation, dressage and cones] the harness should be in good condition, clean and safe, and also uniform in appearance.' This means that you can use one of the webbing sets of harness now on the market, or an ordinary working set. However, this is the cause of some altercation. A few judges tend to forget what the rule book says on the subject and give a slightly lower mark for working harness. If you are unable to afford a good leather set of harness then use whatever you have. You might lose some marks but, with luck, you will be judged only on its cleanliness and fit.

If you do only have a webbing or ordinary working set of harness, this is no reason not to turn up at an event with it as clean as possible. Whether the buckles are chrome or brass, they will look considerably better for a polish with some kind of metal polish. Various parts of the webbing will also benefit from a small amount of Scuff Coat or some such liquid polish. Although, obviously, you cannot put a shine on the webbing, it will enhance the colour.

We shall assume that you have a leather set. The leather harness that you think is clean needs at least another four hours' work on it! To maintain good marks for presentation, it is advisable to use one set of harness for the presentation and one for the marathon. Once you have worked up a good shine on a set of harness, the last thing you want to do is to get it covered with mud and sweat on the marathon and then have to shine it all again from scratch for your next competition. Needless to say, I used my made-to-measure set of English harness for both presentation and marathon for the whole of my first season. It did no lasting damage to the harness but it cost me countless hours' more work than should have been necessary.

The correct fit of harness

The first thing to look at is the fit. You might be sure that everything is as perfect as you can make it – nothing too tight or too loose. However, be prepared to have faults found with the fit by almost every judge you meet. Do not be upset, and get things altered straightaway. Each judge will have a pet hate of some sort. They will pick on everyone's breeching one day and the bridle the next. Once the same fault has been pointed out by several judges, have something permanent done about it. For the fit of the harness to be correct you must have a spare hole to use on every single strap on the harness. Nothing must be on the last hole. You can easily see to this yourself with a hole punch or a quick trip to your saddlers and it should cost you nothing.

The curb chain must not be too tight or too loose. Do not have any spare links on it either. When attaching it to the near-side clip, first get it straight, then put the *underside* of the link onto the clip. If you get it right the chain will lie flat and not be twisted. On many curb chains you will find a round link in the middle that hangs below the rest of the chain; this must be removed as it is only for use with the ridden horse.

54

How to clean your harness

The outside of the harness is the part most looked at, and the bits that have not been given enough polish can be spotted easily. For your harness to be clean is one thing but for it to shine is another.

The leather

I used to spend hours working in saddle soap on both the inside and the outside of the harness – *wrong!* You should *never* use saddle soap on the outside of the harness. You must remove all traces of saddle soap and grease from the outside and start to build up layers of polish. You can buy special harness polish, but it is just the same thing as ordinary shoe polish. When the harness is totally clean on the outside, put a little polish on a rag and work it into the leather. Do not put on a lot or you will not be able to make it shine. When you have put this fine layer of polish onto the leather, and it has dried, take a soft *brush* and polish as though your harness was a shoe. Do not use a cloth to do the polishing as this will leave little bits of fluff behind. With each session of polishing you will need to use less and less polish. You will soon have a permanent sheen that will only need a quick brushing to bring it up to a high gloss.

The inside of the harness can be cleaned in the usual manner, and you can feed the leather from this side. Wipe the inside with warm water then rub in the saddle soap. This will protect the harness and keep it soft and supple.

The fittings

The brass, stainless steel or chrome fittings on the harness all need to shine so that you can see your face in them. When you first polish the metalwork it will take a very long time, but as with the leather, the job will become easier as you build up a good layer. Most makes of brass polish will leave a white mark on any leather they come in contact with, and a white mark on any leather will lose you points. Harglitt brass polish is made specially for this job. It comes in six colours and you will find it for sale at many events, or can order it from the manufacturer.

Brass will tarnish very quickly. If you take your harness to events in a trunk, then it will tarnish even more. To avoid this, pack the harness in newspaper and try to clean it the day before an event.

Then, with luck, all you will have to do on site is give it a quick rub over.

The trap

There are no rules about the type of trap you should use for presentation, except that it must have reflectors on the back which conform with the Highway Code. As with everything in the presentation, it must shine. The best way to get a good deep shine on the paintwork of your trap is to use a spray-on car wax or a domestic furniture polish. You want to be able to see your face in every part of the trap, wheels, shafts, the lot. There is no substitute for hard work here.

As you try to get your trap to shine you are bound to notice parts that have had the paint knocked off. Get out the paint straightaway and touch up these parts. We have even used a large marker pen on the wheel rims to cover up scratches. It will not shine but it does cover up those annoying marks that are bound to occur on a trap in constant use.

If your shafts are covered in a heavy-duty PVC wrap, and this looks dull in the places that get most wear, you can use liquid Scuffcoat shoe polish. This will build up quite a thick coat in time, but it is very easy to wash off after an event. You will then only need to put it on for the presentation.

One part of the trap that you might not think will be examined is the rubber floor mat. This must also shine and be free of mud and grass. To ensure this, have two mats, one for everyday use and one just for the presentation. When you go to get into the trap for the presentation, it is a good idea to climb in in your stocking feet, having already placed clean shoes in the trap, which you can then put on while you are sitting there.

Your trap will be judged not only on its appearance, but also on how it sits on the horse while you are in it. It might be a good idea to ask a knowledgeable friend to look at you sitting in the trap at home when your horse is in the shafts with its best harness on. Get all the straps set to the right hole at this stage. An additional wedge cushion for the whip is most useful for making that person look taller and

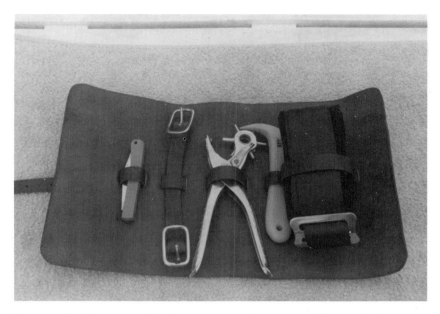

Spares and roll-up spares kit. A very neat and easy way to keep and show your spares. (Bellcrown Equestrian)

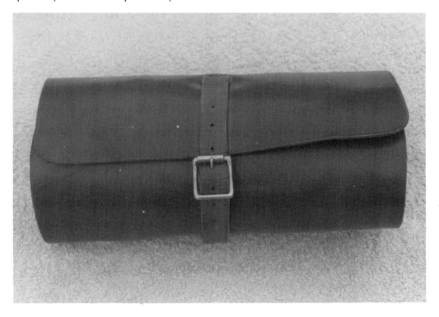

elegant, so this should also be used in this trial set up to make sure everything is as it will be in the competition.

You must also attach your number to the trap. Most people fix it on the back of one of the seats, using PVC insulation tape. You can buy this wonderful stuff in almost any colour. I think that the driving world must keep the manufacturers in business; no one turns up at any event without it.

Lamps

The carrying of some kind of lamp is obligatory but you do not have to use carriage lamps. A pair of period lamps (even modern replicas) can cost from £150 upwards. You will comply with the rules if you use bicycle lamps, as long as they can be seen from both front and back and will work.

If you do have a pair of carriage lamps, you must make sure that the wicks of both candles have been burnt. They should look as though they have been used. Because you need to carry the lamps during the dressage test, and the ground for this can be very bumpy, it is as well to have a strap on each lamp to secure it to the bracket. Most lamps have a metal loop for this purpose.

Spares

You must also carry spares for the presentation. If a full collar is used then you must have a spare hame strap. Everyone must also have a rein or rein splice (and punch) and also a spare trace. These must sparkle as well. Make sure that the trace you carry fits the turnout you are driving, as from time to time this will be checked on a random basis and it will probably be you who gets caught. It is possible to buy a special spares kit, but as with most things in the driving world they come at quite a price. To save some money and gain points you can make your own holder for spares. This looks just like a jewellery or make-up roll.

Whip and groom

What you wear is every bit as important as what your horse wears. If the whip is a lady then the cheapest and easiest way to dress is in a matching shirt and jacket. Try, if possible, to choose a colour that complements your horse. Thomas is blue and white so I wear grey. It is better to chose a simple trilby-style hat. This is easy to keep looking nice, is very business-like in appearance and will not fly off at the first puff of wind – a bit of fine elastic underneath your hair at the back can be a help here. A lady whip must wear a hairnet unless her hair is so short that it does not show.

If the whip is a man then a dark suit and black or brown lace-up shoes are the only things to wear. He can wear a trilby or black or brown bowler depending on what colour the suit is. It might sound daft to mention the shoes but these are also examined. If the whip is a lady then the footwear must be simple; a good stout walking shoe or plain loafer type will do. Whatever either person uses, like everything else, it must shine. Do not wear boots. Some people do wear boots, but we were told by Stella Hancock that this is not considered correct. You might escape detection for a while, then someone will see them and bang goes a point.

The whip must also wear an apron. These come in a variety of colours and materials. Again, choose one that complements the colour you are wearing. I have a black wool one, a very stupid buy as it is always covered in Tom's grey hairs! You can buy them in a gaberdine-type material which not only rejects hairs but is also shower-proof.

The whip must also wear *brown* leather gloves. It makes no difference what colour anything else is, these *must* be brown. It is also a good idea to have a pair of string or woollen gloves in the trap with you. The rules say that string or woollen gloves are to be worn in case of rain as they will not slip on the reins. I put them on the seat and sit on them so that the ends just show. A fresh-flower buttonhole is a nice touch, but this may only be worn by the whip.

If you can afford it, buy a holly whip. They are much lighter to hold than most synthetic whips and definitely look better. However, whatever whip you have it must be able to reach the horse's shoulder when you are sitting in the correct position.

The groom, if a man, must also wear a suit, preferably a dark one with a black bowler. He must wear lace-up shoes with black or brown socks, and also gloves. These do not have to be any special colour. He does not wear an apron or rug. A male groom may also wear full riding kit as described below.

If the groom is a girl then you have a choice of outfits. She can wear a simple skirt/jacket, trousers/jacket or white breeches, white shirt, stock and black jacket accompanied by either a riding hat or black bowler. If she wears a skirt and jacket then a trilby-style hat is best. She is the only person who can wear boots, which must be long black riding boots to fit in with the rest of the riding apparel. She must also wear gloves of some kind and a hairnet unless her hair is so short that it does not show.

If you decide not to have a groom but a passenger instead, then the rules are slightly different. The passenger must use a rug thrown over his/her knees. When the person sitting next to the whip becomes a passenger instead of a groom, he or she *does not* dismount from the trap during the presentation as the groom would.

Manners and etiquette for the presentation

The night before, make sure that you know what time you are on and *where* the presentation for your class takes place. There will often be two sets of judging taking place at the same time. Work out beforehand just how you are going to drive to this point avoiding all the mud (it invariably rains the night before).

Check again in the morning that nothing has been altered, i.e. your start time or place.

Martin and I have now worked out a finely-timed routine. Martin gets the trap out of the lorry and gives it a final polish and fits the lamps. While he does that I give Tom his final brush and take out his bunches. I also like to have enough time to give the brass a quick rub over. Then I put the harness on Tom while Martin puts on his suit. As soon as Martin is ready we both put Tom into the trap. Martin and a temporary groom then drive him around *avoiding* the mud while I change for the presentation.

When you get to the judging area, make sure that the steward knows you have arrived and are ready. You are more than likely to be approached by a steward with a clipboard, who will then check you off on a list, but it does no harm to make yourself known.

Try not to get in the way of anyone about to do their dressage or

…vell-known judge Sarah Garnett letting us know that Tom's mane is on the …g side at Cirencester

…ive too close to the dressage arena and thus distract the person …e ring. For the same reason, also keep a fair distance from the …entation judges.

…is up to the groom to keep an eye on the presentation judges and …he whip when they are ready for you. Before you drive up to the …es, take a look at the ground. If there is a slight slope on it, then …t your horse's head uphill. The horse will then be in draught …ng the judging and all the harness should hang correctly. …hing is more frustrating than a judge thinking that the harness does not fit correctly because you are standing downhill and everything is hanging loose.

When you are asked to come forward, *smile* and walk your horse into place. Halt the horse and make it stand still before the groom gets down. The groom must dismount *backwards* and stand facing the horse's head. The groom should not hold the bridle unless the horse misbehaves. He or she must simply stand there and try to look happy, not bored. For some reason, most of us appear to lose the ability to speak when we are surrounded by judges, becoming as rigid as a poker and unable to answer the simplest questions. The more tense you are, the more likely your horse is to fidget, running the risk of losing a point or, more important, not being relaxed for the dressage test. It is a good idea to teach your horse to allow a foot to be picked up while in harness as the judge is more than likely to ask to see a foot to make sure the horse is well shod.

The judges will prowl around and make you feel very uncomfortable. They will check every buckle and strap to make sure everything is 100 per cent.

If the judges tell you the faults they have found, do ask them how to rectify these faults for next time. As I said before, make sure that more than one judge thinks something is wrong before you have expensive things altered, but do ask them how to improve. Many novice drivers appear to be rather in awe of the judges and never ask for help and advice. That is what they are there for, so do talk to them.

When the judging is finished, take your time in letting the groom remount (as he or she must) before you leave the area. Make your horse walk away in a lively manner as you are still under the judge's eye. In fact, he or she will probably be deciding on your overall appearance as you walk off.

5 Dressage

The dressage test is a nightmare until you learn how to approach it. Every horse is capable of performing a dressage test. True, some will do it far better than others.

The importance of your dressage cannot be stressed too much. A horse that is quick to respond to commands in the dressage arena, and is supple enough to turn corners in a balanced manner, is going to do far better for you in the hazards than one that is stiff and unresponsive. You only need to look at the score board at a competition to see that the people who drive a good dressage test are more likely to be among the winners at the end of the day. Louise Ruff, who excels in the open single-horse class, is a prime example of this. She is always a long way in front in points after the dressage. Louise then drives a good safe marathon and, although she is not the fastest through the hazards, her very good dressage score usually puts her too far in front to be caught up.

There is no great secret in how to achieve a passable test. Like everything else with animals, if you practise things in the right manner, for long enough and with enough praise, your horse will learn.

The first time I did a test with Thomas I was so frightened that as I reached the first halt my mind was a total blank. I broke the first rule and asked my groom for help. (You are not allowed to talk to your groom or passenger at any time while you are in the dressage arena or driving through the cones.) Through clenched teeth Martin told me what the first movement was and as soon as I had Tom moving up the centre line everything came back in a rush and we got through the test. I say 'we got through' our first test – all we managed for the first season was to 'get through' our dressage. It was just something that got in the way of the marathon driving – 'the exciting part of the competition'.

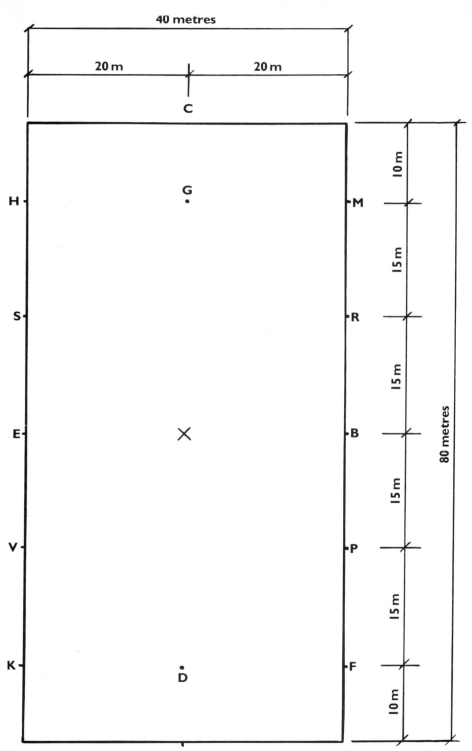

The dressage arena for a single horse or pony. The measurements on the outside of the arena show how it is marked up when the arena is built. The letters at the edge of the arena are displayed on metal stands. The letters D, G and X are represented by sawdust to help the driver work to the correct points during the test

During a conversation with the late Stella Hancock, we said how much we hated the dressage, that it was a bit of a waste of time in our opinion. She reacted very helpfully to our criticisms and pointed out how very important it is and that the only way to succeed in competitive carriage driving is to take dressage lessons and learn the art from scratch. I only wish we had taken her advice to heart and had lessons sooner. It is the one thing it is well worth spending money on because all your driving stems from the dressage. The comment most frequently made about our test was that when Thomas had woken up, about halfway through the test, we gave a passable performance. We struggled on for the first season, slowly learning how to halt and rein back, but our circles were always pear-shaped.

It was not until we took a weekend course with Sarah Garnet that we were shown not only where we went wrong but how to correct these faults.

We were shown how to teach Thomas to trot a true circle and also how to correct his silly faults, like dropping a shoulder on the corners and leaping into trot with such enthusiasm that we almost fell out backwards. I can honestly say that it was money well spent and we have reaped the benefits ever since.

The gaits

Before you start driving a dressage test, you need to know what is expected of you, what gaits the judge is looking for in the horse and what he or she expects to see from the driver.

The walk

It does not matter what speed your horse walks at but it must be an active, rhythmical walk and the horse must be on the bit. The judge will want to see that you have a contact with the bit and that the horse is working, not just slouching along. You must aim to have the hindlegs engaged, with good hock action in a brisk marching type of gait.

The trot

For the novice test you only need to work in two types of trot. When you get into the open classes you have to distinguish three different types. The novice gaits are working trot and extended trot. For the latter you are only asked to show a few lengthened strides. In the open classes you also have to perform a collected trot.

Working trot

This gait should be mastered before the collected trot. In working trot the horse, not yet ready or trained for collected movement, shows itself properly balanced. With a supple poll and remaining on the bit, it goes forward with even, elastic steps and good hock action.

Collected trot

In this gait the horse's steps are shorter but its action is lighter and more mobile than in the working trot. The neck is raised, thus enabling the shoulders to move with greater ease in all directions, the hocks being well engaged and maintaining energetic impulsion, notwithstanding the slower movement.

Extended trot

In this gait the horse covers as much ground as possible with each stride. It therefore lengthens its stride, remaining on the bit with a light contact. The neck is extended, resulting in greater impulsion from the hindquarters. The horse uses its shoulders, covering more ground at each step without the action becoming higher.

Not only must you drive an accurate test on the ground, but you should also give your horse the correct aids. When you first learned to drive it is likely that you were taught to hold the reins in the left hand, with the whip in your right hand. This is what you must do in the dressage test. You will collect more points for this than using the two-handed method.

The judge will also want to see the driver sitting up straight with his or her back against the seat and the reins held close to the body, and with the whip at an angle of 45 degrees across the body.

As you can see from the score sheet, each part of the test is split into separate movements. Each movement is given a mark out of ten.

The scale of marks is
as follows:

10	Excellent		5	Sufficient
9	Very Good		4	Insufficient
8	Good		3	Fairly bad
7	Fairly Good		2	Bad
6	Satisfactory		1	Very bad
			0	Not performed

MOVEMENT		TO BE JUDGED	Mark 0 - 10	REMARKS
1. A X XCH	Enter at working trot Halt Salute Working trot	Driving in on straight line.Transition. Standing straight on bit. Transition,Impulsion,Regularity,Position.		
2. HXF	Change rein & show a few lengthened strides	Impulsion,Regularity,Quality of lengthening		
3. FAK	Working trot	Impulsion,Regularity,Position		
4. K KE	Circle right 20m diameter Working trot	Impulsion,Regularity,Accuracy of figure		
5. EX XB	1/2 circle right 20m diameter 1/2 circle left 20m diameter	Impulsion,Regularity,Accuracy of figure		
6. BM M	Working trot Circle left 20m diameter	Impulsion,Regularity,Accuracy of figure		
7. MCH	Working trot	Impulsion,Regularity,Position		
8. HSPF	Walk	Transition to walk,Regularity, Impulsion,Position		
9. FADX	Working trot	Impulsion,Regularity,Position		
10. X	Halt 10 secs.immobility Rein back 4 paces	Transition,Immobility,Straightness Straightness & Regularity		
11. XG G	Walk Halt Salute Leave Arena at working trot	Transitions,Straightness, Standing on bit		
12. Paces		Regularity.Freedom, Maintenance of paces		
13. Impulsion		Free forward movement		
14. Obedience Lightness		Response to aids,Willing and without resistance		
15. Driver		Use of aids. Handling of whip and reins. Position on box. Accuracy of figures		

Signature of Judge ....

Total .....

Horse Driving Trials Novice Dressage Test No. 7. (This test and No. 5 are the most commonly used tests at the majority of events.) For Singles and Pairs: 80 × 40 m; for Teams and Tandems 100 × 40 m

At the bottom of the sheet there is a separate place for marks for the whip/driver, gaits, impulsion, obedience and lightness.

Teaching your horse the basic dressage gaits

If you have the ability to ride your horse and know how to school under saddle then half your battle has already been won. For those of you who can only drive, there is no doubt that you have a harder job, but with perseverance you should be able to achieve a lot in a couple of months.

When you first start driving out to get your horse fit, make sure that every drive is a lesson. Your horse must learn to obey your voice. The moment you ask it to walk on it must obey you immediately. In other words, it must be paying attention throughout.

Walking off from the halt

Let us take it from the halt. Make sure your horse is standing well to begin with, that the ears are pricked and that it is listening and waiting for your first command. Take up a firm, yet light contact with the bit, have your whip in your right hand, call the horse's name and ask it to walk on. If you get a sloppy response and it starts to amble along, bring it right back to the halt. Do the same thing again, but this time give a crack of the whip as you ask for the walk. If the horse gives you another sluggish response, go back to the halt and get ready again. On this third attempt, give a quick flick with the whip on the rump.

No matter how many times you have to repeat this first step, do not get cross or lose your temper. The most important thing is to give lots of praise as soon as the horse does correctly what you have asked it to do.

When you have achieved the 'take off' into a walk that satisfies you do not then sit back and let the horse plod along just because it has done it correctly. Now that you have taught the horse how to walk off from the halt in an active fashion you must maintain this activity in the walk. Keep using your voice all the time to chivvy the horse along, at the same time remembering to praise it if it keeps up a lively pace.

To begin with, keep things simple and just practise coming to the halt and walking off in the correct manner. As you should be teaching this first dressage lesson at the beginning of your training programme you can tie it in with your walking fitness programme, which, if you remember, is all you should ask your horse to do during the first two weeks.

Progressing to working trot

As you come to the beginning of your third week's training, you can also begin to teach your horse its second dressage lesson – how to perform an active working trot. All you have to do for the transition from walk to trot is repeat the first lesson from halt to walk.

Make sure that you have a good contact with the bit and that the horse is in a smart walk, call its name and ask it to 'Trot on', giving plenty of emphasis on the 'T'. Try to make your voice bright, with some life in it. The horse should find this invitation to move faster hard to resist.

You are not just asking the horse to go faster, though, you are now trying to make it use itself properly. The working trot is a horse's natural gait for covering the ground; it is its most efficient gait and the one that tires it least.

That may be fine for everyday driving, but when the horse performs in the dressage arena, it must put more energy into it. Do not let the horse hang on the bit; use your voice and a little more contact on the bit than you would normally use to make it use its hindquarters more efficiently. You need the horse to develop a bounce in its stride.

Extended trot

To develop the extended trot is much harder. Unless your horse will extend naturally, you will find that as you push it on it will probably only go faster but not lengthen its stride. You will only really achieve an extension once you have taught your horse to collect. In the novice class a collected trot is not required, but as you need to show a few lengthened strides you will, in fact, need to teach the horse a small amount of collection. A good way to do this from the ground is either to long-rein or lunge your horse in a 20-m circle. Mark a point on the circumference of the circle and then count how many paces are required to reach this marker. If you are using long-reins, simply apply a little more pressure on the reins and urge the horse on with your voice.

It will take a couple of circuits of the circle before the horse shortens its stride. You can check this by again counting how many paces are needed to get round the 20 m. You should find that if your horse goes round this circle in, say, 20 paces, you should, with some practice, be able to increase this to 25 paces or so. Once you have achieved this it will then be much easier to ask him to trot on and in this way he should learn to extend slightly.

If you are unable to long-rein, try the same exercise sitting up in the trap. Collect your horse up, make it shorten its stride and when it has done so for, say, 20 m (20 yd) push it on. As it reaches working trot, keep your contact on the reins but push the horse a little more with your voice and with practice it should learn to extend for you. This can be a good point at which to have a lesson with an expert.

As you work on the gaits, make sure that you can change these at a given marker. In the dressage test every change of gait or direction is made as soon as the horse's nose reaches the appropriate marker on the side of the arena. I find a good way to practise this is to choose a lamppost or gateway and decide to halt at that point. With practice you will learn how much warning your horse needs either to halt or change gait. You are looking to make these transitions appear very smooth to the judges. You do not want your horse to fall into a walk or jump into a trot. Only practice will give you results. If you make every drive a lesson your horse will not become as bored as it would if you work constantly in a school. I am sure that most people are like me and do not have access to a school anyway. We do not even have any flat ground in our fields; they are all on a slope.

The rein back
When you have mastered the gaits and transitions, the next step is to teach your horse to rein back. In ridden dressage this movement is only asked of the advanced horse. The ridden horse has the advantage of the rider's legs to help it, and without blinkers it can also see

where it is going. Most people who have only driven for pleasure have probably never taught their horses to rein back for fear of a tip-up.

I do not know if there is a textbook that describes how to teach your horse to back in some approved fashion, but I will tell you how I teach my horses, as this method has worked for me. I think the reason why so many horses will not rein back is quite simply because they cannot see what is behind them.

Many of us have seen other competitors asking for rein back only to see horses rear up so sharply that they almost fall over backwards. This is because the drivers have not taken the time to teach the horses gently and quietly from day one how to go back.

From the first day a young horse spends in my stable I push it on the chest every time I go into the box and ask it to go back. After a few weeks it learns the command and will move away on request.

Once it understands the command, I take it into the field in a head collar with a lead rope, stand by its side and ask it to back. I do not mind at this point if it backs at an odd angle, as long as it trusts me and moves in the right direction. Once the horse is happy with me by its side, I progress to an ordinary bridle and long-reins.

When I am confident that the horse is relaxed about the command coming from behind it, I change to a driving bridle. During the first driving lesson with blinkers, try to progress one step at a time. Do not forget the horse can no longer see you and will need to be assured that it is still quite safe. Eventually it will back for the required number of steps, walking and not shuffling. Now you can go on to teach the horse how to go back in a straight line.

You will probably find that each horse tends to favour one side more than the other. Try standing it with a fence on the side to which it tends to swing out. Because it trusts you not to let it hurt itself, it will not take fright should it touch the fence.

The first time you try this in the trap, make sure that you are on very flat ground, preferably, even, facing uphill on a slight downward slope, so that the horse does not feel the weight of the trap during these first attempts. On approaching a main road where there is a white stop-line, I sometimes pretend that the road markings are the X in the arena and practise a rein back. However, do not overdo the rein back once the horse has learned it, because you only want it

71

to do it when you ask for it and the horse will soon begin to anticipate your command.

How to drive a circle

This is, I think, one of the hardest things to do until you are shown the simple method Sarah Garnet used at our weekend course. It is most important that you find some flat ground to practise on. Take four road-warning-type cones and place them at the four opposite points of an imaginary 30-m circle. Once you can drive around this area happily and do not cut the corners, you can slowly reduce this diameter to give a 20-m circle. When you can drive this with the cones, progress to driving a 20-m circle without the use of cones. Remember to work on both reins equally.

Putting a test together

Now that you can drive all the separate movements of the test, you need to know how to put it all together. If, like most of us, you do not have access to a 40 × 80-m arena, then the following will assist in simulating one. First, using pen and paper, copy out, preferably to scale, an arena complete with its marker letters and their dimensions apart. Any flat (or almost flat) field of sufficient size can be used as follows. Pace out your 40 × 80-m area, using natural objects as your markers where possible (in the absence of real markers). Learn to follow the line of your circles etc. on foot and, when committed to memory, drive an imaginary test. Both you and your horse will benefit from this exercise.

However, if you practise the test you are to perform shortly before the event, your horse will learn it sooner than you think and will begin to cut the corners and rein back before you ask it to. I had that experience with Tom and had a real fight to keep him from galloping through the test.

Before I go on to tell you how I learn a test and how to salute, let me stress the point that all the things explained above are simply the same movements required in the marathon and hazards and in everyday driving. If your horse will rein back in a straight line you are going to be able to unhook yourself from a post without having to put a groom down. If your horse will move off into a smart bouncy trot on command, it is not going to lose time in a hazard when you have had to drop into walk to get through a tight corner.

Learning the test

I learn the test by getting several sheets of paper and writing down each movement with the gaits marked in different colours. The illustrations on page 80 show how to build up a test using this method. I learn one sheet at a time until I am sure the whole test is built up in my mind in sections. I then practise the test by walking through it in my imagination as I cook the dinner or mow the lawn. This method is of even greater use when you progress to the open test as it is so much longer. The novice tests are short and although they are easy to learn (there are, at present, only three tests) they can be harder to drive because your horse does not have time to settle down before the end of the test.

When you arrive at an event, make sure that you find the arena you are to perform in and walk through the test a couple of times on foot. Use trees or buildings to help you get a bearing for your circles etc. You must walk through your test before any of the dressage has started because once the arenas are in use you will not be able to walk on them, not even during the judges' coffee break.

The salute

Do not hurry the salute; it looks like very poor manners to rush through it.

A lady driver (the driver is usually called the whip) looks straight

The following pages illustrate the lady's salute

A lady whip's salute

i)   Put the reins securely into the left hand
ii) Raise the whip horizontally until level with your eyes and hold for a count of two
iii) Keeping the whip in the horizontal position, lower your head. Count to three, then raise your eyes to the level of the whip again. Return the whip hand to the normal position

ahead with her head held quite still. She then raises the whip horizontally in front of her eyes, holds it at this point for a count of three and at the same time dips her head and then returns her eyes to the level of the whip. The whip is then returned to her waist.

A gentleman driver must first transfer the whip into his left hand along with the reins. He then takes hold of his bowler hat in his right hand and removes it completely. He holds out the bowler for a count of three, then returns it to his head and takes back the whip.

The following pages illustrate the gentleman's salute

A gentleman whip's salute

i)   Put the whip into the left hand
ii) Take off your hat and lower it in your right hand with the crown of the hat facing forwards
iii) Lower your head for a count of three. Replace your hat and take the whip back into your right hand

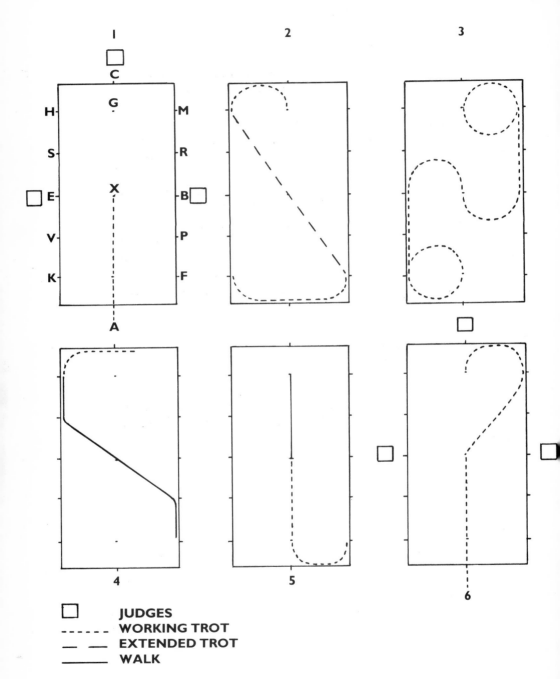

JUDGES
WORKING TROT
EXTENDED TROT
WALK

Dressage Test No. 7, movements 1–11. The arena letter markers as shown on Diagram 1 are the same for Diagrams 1–6. Diagram 6 demonstrates how to leave the arena in a neat and tidy manner. The judges will continue to watch you until you have left the arena

Driving the test

When your turn comes, give your horse plenty of time to take in the surroundings. All horses are different, some need a long hard work-in before a test; others only become excited if they trot around too much. One of the things you are trying to show in your test is that although your horse is very fit for the marathon, it is obedient and willing and you are able to keep its energy under check before the marathon.

A horn will sound as your signal to enter the arena. Give yourself room and time to set yourself up to enter the arena in a straight line. You have one minute from the sound of the bell before you have to start your test. A minute is a long time, so do not hurry. Use the time to make a dead straight approach. When you have completed your test, you are still under the judge's eye until you have left the arena. The diagram opposite shows how to leave the arena in the correct manner.

Points to remember

Take your time before entering the arena.
Do not rush your salute.
If a move goes wrong, forget it and set yourself up for the next one.
Most importantly, smile, take deep breaths and look relaxed and
   happy!

6   The Marathon

There can be no doubt that this is the part of competitive carriage driving most enjoyed by both horse and driver. When your horse has been to a couple of events, it will soon learn where the marathon comes in the timetable and its excitement will be very noticeable.

Roughly speaking, the number of penalty points that you can collect on the marathon section is more than the other three sections put together. So the amount of time spent working out your times for the marathon and the routes through the hazards is never wasted. You cannot spend too much time doing this.

The marathon is the only part of a competition where the groom's assistance is allowed, not to mention essential. For the novice driver the marathon is in three stages.

Section A

The maximum distance is 10 km (6¼ miles), although this may vary slightly, and the maximum average speed required to cover this in the time allowed is 15 kmph (9 mph). Trot used to be compulsory for all of this section, but the rules have now been changed and any gait is permitted. If you come in after the time allowed, you collect penalty points. You may come in two minutes before the time allowed, but any time before those two minutes will also give you penalty points.

Section B or D

In a full marathon these two sections are performed at a walk. In a novice marathon, it will depend on the way the marathon is set out which of the walks the novice driver will complete. The distance is up to 1200 m and the maximum average speed is 7 km/hr for horses and 6 km/hr for ponies. Again, you may come in before the time given, but you will collect 0·2 penalty points for each second or part of a second over that time.

At the end of the walk there is a compulsory halt, when your horse may be checked by a vet to make sure that it has recovered from section A. If your horse is deemed unfit by the vet he will advise an official to pull you out of the competition at this point.

Section E

This is the part you have been working towards, really the most exciting and challenging part of the whole competition – the hazard section of the marathon. Now is the time when your horse's fitness will really be tested. It will already have covered about 11 km, most of it at almost full stretch and some of the distance across undulating ground. The maximum distance for Section E is 10 km (6¼ miles) and the maximum average speed is 15 kmph (9 mph) but you must travel faster than this because of the time you will lose in the hazards. You may complete this section as early as you wish, but penalty points will be collected for a *late* finish. As in section B/D one second or part of a second merits 0·2 penalty points.

Working out times

The time for Section A is usually easy to gauge as each kilometre has a marker. This is where clipboard and paper are needed. Write down precisely at what time each kilometre should be reached, and use this as a quick and reliable check on your timing.

Make sure that your stop-watch is really securely attached in a position close to hand where it cannot be accidentally stopped by a sudden jolt. Check your start time with the timekeeper and set a wrist watch to the official time.

To persuade your horse to walk at 7 kmph (4⅓ mph) average speed sounds very easy, but take my word for it, a great deal of patient urging will be needed to complete within the time allowed.

For Section E, you will have to check the time allowed, then make

certain you give yourself enough time to get through the hazards –
say, 50 seconds for each hazard.

Planning hazard routes

The secret of good hazard driving is the time spent in working out
routes. Give yourself lots of time to study the hazards and do not be
influenced by other drivers when they say they only need to walk
them a couple of times. If you consider that you need to walk each
hazard six times then do just that.

I look at the hazards in the correct order as I get confused if I look
at Number 5 and then Number 1. It might mean more leg work but
it helps to put the hazards in the correct pattern in your mind. This is
important and there is no shortcut.

The way that some hazards are built can be very deceptive to the
eye. You might be certain that a gap is too small for you to get
through or vice versa. It can be a help to carry a stick that is the same
width as your vehicle. You can then place the stick on the ground at
an awkward turn and use it to work out exactly how to get through.

Other drivers, who are looking at a hazard at the same time as
you, might decide to go through a gap that you have just convinced
yourself is too small. Do not forget that they might be driving a pair
(which can sometimes get round tighter turns than a single horse
because of the use of a four-wheel vehicle), or be driving a tiny,
nippy pony. You know your horse better than anyone else, so only
you know what it can do.

When you pick your route, try to choose one that you will be able
to keep moving on even if the distance on the ground is longer. For
example, see the illustration of the Slippery Slope at Castle Howard
1988.

People who chose Route A here were very lucky to get round the
turn after Gates A and B. Several people we watched had to abandon
one turn or the other and also wasted a lot of time trying to perform
these two very tight turns.

Route B was a much quicker way of reaching Gate B but again the
right-hand turn was very tight between the tree and the post and rail.
Also, this turn led down a steep and slippery bank. Many people

The Slippery Slope at Castle Howard, 1988. This diagram shows how the ground falls away at each side of the hazard. It gives the impression that the safest way to drive it is staying on the top of the bank. A, B and C are the three Gates of the hazard to be negotiated

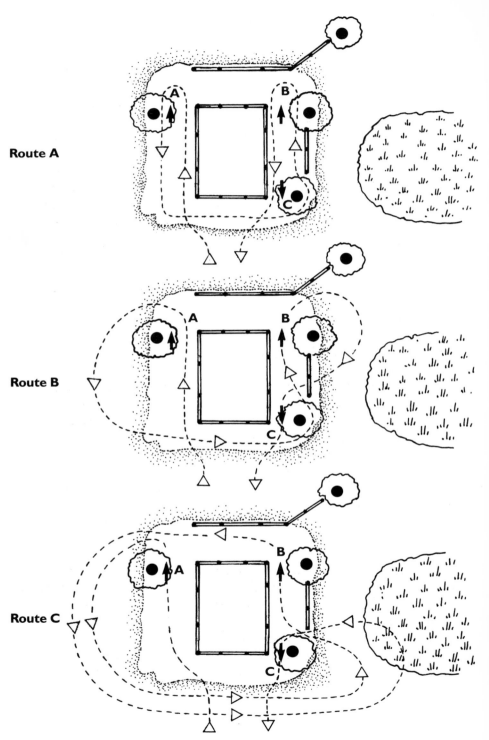

Route A

Route B

Route C

The Slippery Slope at Castle Howard illustrating three routes in one hazard

wasted time either by getting hooked up on the tree, or by having to change the turn into a left-handed one to follow the last part of Route C.

Route C was much longer on the ground but the horses could keep up a constant trot and even canter between Gates A and B and again between B and C. This is a good example of a longer flowing route.

You will find that you go faster in the hazards if you can keep up a good trot rather than having to stop to unhook yourself because you tried to cut too many corners. Do remember that your shafts stick out in front of your horse's shoulders, so allow that little bit of extra room to get them around a corner. Our thanks go to Fred and Beryl Pendlebury who pointed out that Tom, not a wiry lightweight, should be driven more like a pair than a bendy toy. We improved our times and now flow much more in the hazards as we drive the longer routes.

If a hazard is built on a hill, try to work out a route where you stay up on the higher ground once you have gained it. Nothing will tire your horse more than having to pull uphill more than is necessary and you will also lose some of your momentum. Make sure your groom is aware of which way to lean when you have to turn a corner on a hill. Do not let him or her make the mistake of leaning onto the corner as one must on the flat. In this instance he or she must lean *uphill*. (It's not a good idea to lose a groom!)

The two routes at Bathurst Gates, Cirencester 1988 show how the hazards can be very deceptive on paper.

Route A opens out the hazard and ensures freedom of movement for the horses. This route flows, but the hazard was large and much thought had to be given to whether, in this instance, the longer route would be the faster way.

Route B looks to be very tight and twisty. In fact, it drove much faster than it looked. Once you had driven through Gate A, all the rest of the turns were on a left rein. Trying to choose a route that is on the same rein wherever possible is as important as looking for the more open or flowing routes.

When you have made up your mind which route to take, try not to change it as this is a sure way of throwing yourself into total confusion. As there are up to eight hazards, it is not easy to

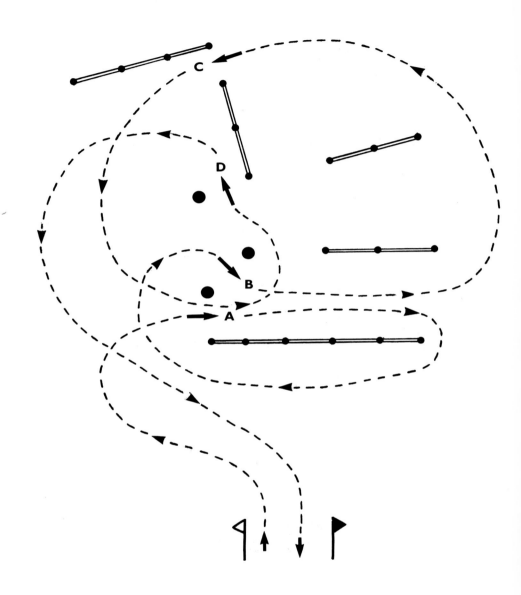

Bathurst Gates, Cirencester 1988
Route A. A, B, C and D are the Gates to be negotiated

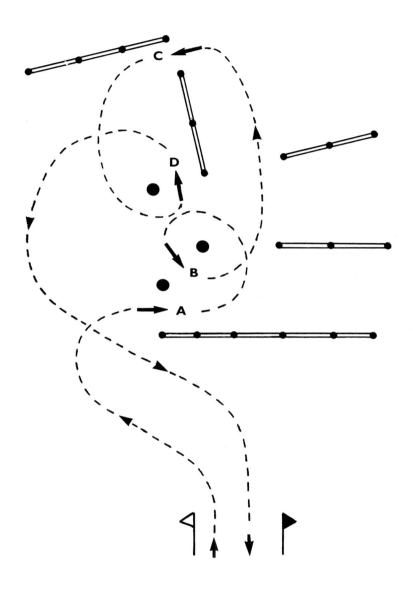

Bathurst Gates, Cirencester 1988
Route B. A, B, C and D are the Gates to be negotiated

remember the route anyway, so the less changing around you do the better.

You may find that some of the routes you have chosen prove too risky. If this is the case, have an escape route worked out. If things do go wrong, do not waste time trying to do the impossible, but change direction and carry on.

One last thing to consider when choosing your route and before you commit it to both paper and memory, is the side your horse may favour when performing a tight turn at trot. If it is more supple on, say, the left rein, then try to choose a route that gives it that advantage. It could save valuable seconds.

Your groom must learn the hazard routes as well so that instant directional help can be given. This is especially necessary to ensure that gates are driven in the correct order. Also, your groom needs to be able to re-route you if you happen to lose your way, as can happen.

You will be provided with maps of all the hazards at national events. When, and only when, you have your final routes worked out, mark them on the maps. The maps will not be much use when you are actually in the hazards (and if you do need to look at them it means you have not spent long enough walking the hazards), but you can run through the hazards with your groom before you start, checking everything against the map in his or her hand. Take the maps with you on the marathon. This is vital in case you forget the route of the hazard you are approaching.

If you have a water hazard to cross and you know your horse is not happy about water, you will have to put your groom down, thus incurring extra penalty points. If you have to go through the water twice, make sure your groom *stays* down until you are finally clear of the water. If he or she remounts for some of the hazard and then has to dismount again, you will collect penalty points *both* times.

The groom must follow the vehicle through each gate of the hazard, as he or she is part of the turnout and you would be eliminated if your groom did not pass through all the gates.

If you do not have access to water at home, you will have to do what I do – drive in the rain and go through as many puddles as possible. If you approach the organisers of an event with a water hazard, they will usually let you practise through it when everyone has completed the course.

On the morning of the marathon

It is a good idea to give your horse its last feed well before your start time. Take four hours as an average and work back from there. I used to feed Tom four hours before the start of a marathon, but through trial and error have found that he does much better with a gap of nearer six hours. Martin usually creeps out at 4 a.m. or so to give this feed! It is not an odd sight to see people in dressing gowns feeding horses at four or five o'clock in the morning so do not think you will be the only fool around at that time of day.

If the going is very muddy and your horse has a long tail it can be a good idea to put the tail up out of the way. This is very simple to do. Put the whole of the tail into one big plait, fasten the end with a rubber band then fold the tail in two. When the tail is folded, fasten it again with another couple of elastic bands and then use some insulation tape over the top of a tail bandage – the tape will not catch the hair of the tail but will stick back onto itself and this arrangement will keep the tail out of the mud.

Some people do this no matter what the going is like. However, if the route passes through a lot of woodland, your horse will need its tail to keep flies away. Decide whether your horse will be more bothered by a tail heavy with mud or by flies and act accordingly.

Use a nylon head collar underneath your bridle in case of a tip-out.

The marathon is the only part of the competition in which you are allowed to use any kind of leg protection on your horse.

What to wear

There is no rule about clothing for the driver or groom but I do recommend skull caps. It only needs a miscalculation in a hazard to smack your head on a tree and knock yourself out. Many people wear matching jumpers and silks on their caps so that friends can easily identify them. This also helps the commentator to identify you in the hazards. Non-slip shoes or boots are also a good idea.

At some time you will find yourself out on the marathon during a cloud burst. Good waterproofs are a must, they not only keep you dry but will keep you warm in a strong wind. You need to stay warm and dry, but if you buy clothes that are too bulky you will find it hard to drive. We have found that light nylon trousers are the best for our legs, while light wax jackets are very good on the top half if they are big enough for a couple of jumpers to fit underneath. You can always remove a jumper during the halt at the end of the walk section so that you can move freely during the hazards.

The last things to check before you set off on the marathon are:

Do you have your number on? (A tabard is required for the number on a marathon – the groom can wear this. It can be bought from the British Horse Society.)

Have you got your stopwatches?

Have you got the maps?

Is there a halter rope in your spares kit?

Are all the spares you need in your trap?

Put in some 'reward' Polos or carrots for your horse to eat at the halt.

Hints on marathon driving

Remember that the course is marked with flags. You must pass *all* of these and in the right direction. Some flags are set out on the course as 'gates' – this is when two flags are set up in a pair – *red on the right and white on the left.* You must pass through all of these gates which will be clearly marked and numbered on your map. If the course has a lot of gates it is a good idea to write the numbers down, say 1 to 60, and cross them off as you pass through them. This can be difficult for the groom to do as well as time keeping, but there is nothing worse than to come in at the end of the marathon with a very good score and find yourself eliminated because you missed out a gate. If you do miss one you can go back and 'clear it' before you pass through the next gate. The rule book is slightly unclear at this point: it does say that the gates must be passed in the correct order, so it is generally taken that if you realise your mistake before you pass the next gate you can go back to the one you missed.

When you reach the ten minutes' compulsory halt you will find a supply of fresh water, buckets and sponges. These are for the use of all drivers; to give your horse a drink and to sponge it off and cool it

Negotiating a hazard at our first event in Trefnant long before we learnt about two-wheeled vehicles and back steps

and help bring down its pulse and respiration. Take care how much water you apply to your horse. On a chilly day, too much cooling could produce some stiffness which might take the next few kilometres to work out. Another way to help bring down the pulse and respiration on a hot sunny day is to let your horse stand in the shade. If no shade is available, place a cold wet towel over the horse's head.

7   Cone Driving

The cones are great fun to drive. You might well find yourself becoming nervous as the time to drive them approaches, but if you learn how to drive them in the same calm manner in which you now drive your dressage test, you will be able to enjoy them. If you enjoy this final part of the competition, so will your horse. If you have spent some time at home getting your eye in for the distance apart the cones are set, this is the only practice you need. The rest will come from the obedience you have taught your horse for the dressage and your ability to choose and memorise the fastest route between cones.

The vehicle you use for the cone driving must be the same one used in the dressage phase.

Rules for cone driving

As these are subject to possible annual amendments, I have not included them. However, a copy of the current rules should be obtained from the British Horse Society Horse Driving Trials Group, as they are lengthy and full understanding of them can help in decision-making, for example whether or not to put a groom down. The vehicle track width for cone driving is specific in the rules and will differ for pony and horse classes. If your vehicle does not have the correct track width, nor an extending axle, hoola hoops (wheel extensions) are permitted in the UK. Scurry bars are no longer permitted.

You may be surprised to learn how and why penalties are awarded (in addition to dislodging the ball from a cone) and what can cause elimination from the event during the cone phase.

Faults incurring penalties include: knocking over cone/ball dislodged, groom dismounting, disobedience, knocking over start or finish flags.

Elimination will result from such faults as: taking the wrong course, starting before the bell, receiving outside assistance (from your groom), driving without a whip in your hand, to name but a few!

Obtain a copy of the rules, learn them and enjoy the cones!

Dress

Hard though it is, you must wear your presentation gear for the cones. I have never yet seen anyone eliminated for not doing so, but judges are becoming much stricter on this matter and it is not worth the risk of being eliminated. In a way, it is a good idea because it encourages you to clean off your trap thoroughly after the marathon. This is especially worthwhile if you only have one vehicle, as most of us do.

Walking the course

The cones are usually open for inspection in plenty of time before the class starts, but, as with the dressage test, you are not allowed to walk the course (and learn the route) once the class has started. You are well advised to give yourself enough time to walk the course at least twice. Not only must you learn the route, but you must also make sure where the start and finish flags are, and how to get to the start without going through any of the obstacles.

As with the hazards, take your time in walking around the arena. Some of the cones may look very easy to negotiate, but take care to check the angle at which they are set. Under the *present* rules, the gaps between the cones are set at 30 cm (12 in) wider than the permissible track width for your class. This means that your wheels, with the spacer hoops fitted, will have 15-cm (6 in) clearance on each side of the trap. This is reasonable room and, with practice, you should find that you can get through the cones clear of any faults. You will only really learn how to walk your cones when you have driven in a couple of events.

As you drive at more events you will learn how quickly your

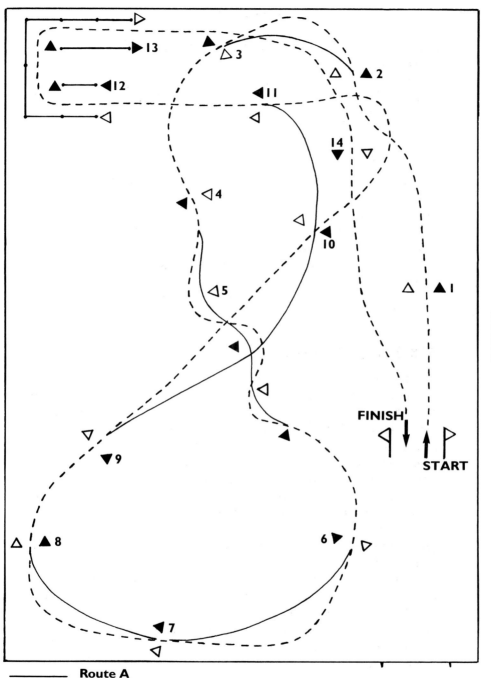

JUDGES

13

12

3

2

11

14

4

10

1

5

FINISH

START

9

8

6

7

—————— **Route A**
- - - - - - **Route B**

Two routes through the cones

horse can turn and how close you can get to a pair of cones before you must set your horse straight. Some ponies can take every pair of cones on an angle, while others must have plenty of room to look at them first. I have given an example of a cone course, showing different ways of driving it. Route A is for a nippy horse or pony with an experienced driver; Route B is for a slightly slower horse with a more novice driver. Both routes will get you round the course in time, but in Route B the driver must make sure that where there is an open stretch of ground, he or she pushes the horse into a much faster trot.

How to drive the cones

Drive the cones in whatever manner is most comfortable for you and your horse. You may hold the reins as you like but *must* carry the whip at all times. If you drop the whip while in the ring you will be eliminated. Make sure that you keep up an active trot until you have passed the finish flags. The stop watch will run until your horse's nose has passed these. When you have passed the finish, you must bring your horse back to a walk and leave the arena at a walk. You will be told off or even run the risk of elimination if you leave the arena at a trot or canter.

You might think, as a novice, that you will be better off going slowly and surely to begin with. The slower you go, however, the more likely you are to knock the cones over. If you go slowly you are giving your horse time to question what you are asking it to do. If you are positive and drive in an active trot, the horse is far more likely to go straight and therefore give you a clear round.

Your score at this part of the competition

As each part of the competition for your class is completed, the score and the places will go up on the master score board. Look carefully at your place and work out how many cones there are between you and the people above and below you. Although you do not want to knock any cones down and collect any more penalty points, it can give you confidence if you know you can still keep your place by knocking down no more than, say, three cones.

If you have been eliminated during some other part of the competition you will still be allowed to take part in the cones. If you can make the effort to do this, you will at least receive a commemorative rosette. It might not be a lot to take home but it does prove that you took part and gives you something to aim for at the next event. Perhaps it will spur you on to greater effort next time.

Your turn

When it is time for your class to begin, you will be sent into the arena in reverse order, i.e. the people who have been eliminated will go in first followed by the person with the highest number of penalty points and so on. Before your turn, make sure that you make use of the practice cones that, more often than not, will have been provided. This gets your horse in the mood and gives you time to 'get your eye in'.

When you enter the ring, approach the judges' box and give them the same salute as you do in the dressage test. At some events you will be told there is no need to salute, but always check with the ring steward before you go into the ring. Just because the person in front of you has not given a salute does not mean that he or she was correct.

After giving your salute, trot your horse around until the starting bell is sounded. However, there is no need to rush through the start flags just because the bell has rung. If you need to do one more circle because you are not quite ready, then do so. You must start within one minute of the bell, however, which is quite enough time to compose yourself and your horse.

Four golden rules

Take time to learn your route well.

Remember to salute the judges.

Wait for the starting bell. Beginning before it rings will result in elimination.

Your groom must not give any help by way of pointing or talking.

99

8 Final Words

This handbook has played on my mind for three years. In the first place this is because I once desperately needed one to find out how to take part in this fascinating sport; latterly because I felt that if I did not write one no one else was going to.

Sarah Garnet, Edwina Hart and the late Stella Hancock all talked about putting their heads together and writing a book like this as a joint effort (I am sure it would have been more comprehensive than mine). Without their unknowing help and advice I do not think I could have sat down and written this. Over the past few seasons, as I have made mistakes, one or the other has politely told me what I was doing wrong. All these points have been used in this book to help you. Credit goes to them and reinforces what I have tried to put across: this is a friendly sport.

A second, very important, fact is that this is also a family sport. Without the help of my husband, Martin, I could never have got beyond first base. While I have been struggling to write this, he has been out in the freezing cold refitting a laundry wagon with a super living area and portable stable. Nicholas, our eleven-year-old son (who cannot stand the work involved with horses, e.g. mucking out) has been out there with him, holding bits of wood and painting. His coffee-making skills have also improved! Anna, who is thirteen, has willingly made a very big sacrifice. She competes with her pony Peter Pan in BSPS working hunter classes, but not during the summer. She misses all the summer shows and has never once complained. Instead, she throws herself into helping us at events and is a regular sight as she dashes from hazard to hazard to watch us and her other favourite competitors. Thank you family.

I think the only drawback is the cost. Unless you and your family are happy to wave goodbye to summer holidays (who wants to go mid-season anyway) and some of the other family treats in life, then you will find it hard to compete on a serious level. It is possible to feel a passing flush of green as someone arrives at a competition with a brand-new lorry and trailer plus smart carriage, but do they have any more fun than you? I don't think so.

My advice is to have a go. Smarten up your trap, wash your horse and get out there. At your first national do not be afraid of going into the beer tent on Saturday evening and talking to people you don't know. If you approach a team or tandem driver who is higher up the ladder than you, remember that that driver realises only too well that he or she could be at the bottom of the class at the next event. We all have two things in common – we enjoy driving our horses; we enjoy meeting each other. With few exceptions we all turn into gypsies for five months, drifting from one event to the next, renewing old friendships and making new ones.

I hope we see you on the circuit.

Further Reading

British Horse Society, *Horse Driving Trials National Rules* (1986)
Coombs, Tom, *Horse Driving Trials* (David & Charles, 1985)
Faudel-Phillips, H., *The Driving Book* (J. A. Allen, 1970)
HRH The Duke of Edinburgh, *Competition Carriage Driving* (Horse Drawn Carriages Limited, Macclesfield, 1982)
Jung, Emil Bernard, *Combined Driving* (J. A. Allen, 1970)
Ryder, Tom, *On The Box Seat* (Horse Drawn Carriages, 1969)
Walrond, Sallie, *Breaking a Horse to Harness* (J. A. Allen, 1989)
—— *A Guide to Driving Horses* (Pelham, 1977)
—— *Your Problem Horse* (Pelham, 1982)

Useful Addresses

Animal Health Trust
Lanway Park
Kennett
Newmarket
Suffolk

Artistic Iron Products
Sparrow Lane
Long Bennington
Newark
Nottinghamshire NG23 5DC

Bellcrown Equestrian
P.O. Box 224
Chester CH3 9OA
Tel: 0829 782505

British Horse Society
Horse Driving Trials Office
The British Equestrian Centre
Stoneleigh
Kenilworth
Warwickshire CV8 2LR
Tel: 0203 52441

The British Driving Society
27 Dugard Place
Barford
Nr Warwick CV35 8DX
Tel: 0926 624420

Don Carney
17 Catherine Street
Macclesfield
Cheshire SK11 6ET

Horse and Hound
Kings's Reach Tower
Stamford Street
London SE1 9LS
Tel: 071 261 6315

Carriage Driving
EPG Publications Ltd
Finlay House
6 Southfield Road
Kineton Road Industrial Estate
Southam
Leamington Spa
Warwickshire CV33 0BR

Tedman Harness
58 Clifden Road
Worminghall
Aylesbury
Buckinghamshire HP18 9JP
Tel: 084 47 318

Epilogue

Since completing the manuscript for this book I have had a total hip replacement. I am now able to ride again and school my horses under saddle for the first time for years. The absence of pain and the freedom to walk normally recommends this kind of surgery to any others who may have doubts about this kind of operation.

Index